THREE SCREENPLAYS

FEDERICO FELLINI

THREE SCREENPLAYS

I Vitelloni

Il Bidone

The Temptations of Doctor Antonio

Translated from the Italian by Judith Green

The Orion Press • *New York*

All rights reserved
Translation© 1970, Grossman Publishers, Inc.
Library of Congress Catalogue Card Number: 74-94090

Manufactured in the United States of America

CONTENTS

I Vitelloni

Credits

An Italo-French co-production
PEG FILMS—CITE FILMS

Story:	Federico Fellini
	Ennio Flaiano
	Tullio Pinelli
Screenplay:	Federico Fellini
	Ennio Flaiano
Production director:	Luigi Giacosi
Production inspector:	Danilo Fallani
Production secretary:	Ugo Benvenuti
Operators:	Otello Martelli
	Luciano Trasatti
	Carlo Carlini
Cameramen:	Roberto Girardi
	Franco Villa
Editing:	Rolando Benedetti
Music:	Nino Rota
Conducted by:	Franco Ferrara

The "Vitelloni"
Moraldo: Franco Interlenghi
Alberto: Alberto Sordi
Fausto: Franco Fabrizi
Leopoldo: Leopoldo Trieste
Riccardo: Riccardo Fellini

The Relatives of the "Vitelloni"
Sandra: Eleonora Ruffo
Fausto's Father: Jean Brochard
Alberto's Sister: Claude Farell
Michele: Carlo Romano
Sandra's Father: Enrico Viarisio
Sandra's Mother: Paola Borboni

The Women of the "Vitelloni"
Michele's Wife: Lida Baarova
The lady in the
  Movie Theater: Arlette Sauvage
Chinese Maiden: Vira Silenti
Chanteuse: Maja Nipora

Other actors: Achille Majeroni
                    Guido Martufi
                    Silvio Bagolini
                    Milvia Chianelli

The film credits appear superimposed on the night view of a street or piazza of a provincial town. From the distance we see four young men approaching, arms linked, singing loudly and gaily.

Kursaal terrace. Outside. Night.

The terrace of the Kursaal, a resort-town café and nightclub, which is crowded this evening for the election of the local beauty queen. The band plays as Riccardo, at the microphone, sings.

VOICE OF RICCARDO *(offscreen, singing):* The mystery of night ... has stolen the light ...

Gusts of wind from the dark sea tear through the bunting and the potted palms and whip the edges of the tablecloths.

The voice of the Speaker now partially covers Riccardo's singing.

VOICE OF SPEAKER: This is the Kursaal of our little city, and we're now in the midst of the last event of the season: the election of Miss Siren of 1953.

Antonio, an elderly waiter, surveys the crowd as if foreseeing a general exodus caused by the bad weather. He looks up at the sky, then goes off among the tables, passing in front of the long table where the jury is seated. The jury is composed of Lilia Randi, a film starlet who has come up from Rome and three gentlemen.

A fan approaches the actress and obtains her autograph.

SPEAKER *(continuing):* It's a fine crowd, isn't it? Italian tourists, foreigners, and even a film actress up from Rome to sit on the jury. Everybody's here, and of course we're here too — the Vitelloni.

From one of the tables, two young men, Alberto and Leopoldo, gaze at the group of contestants for the beauty prize.

SPEAKER: This is Alberto.

Alberto turns to someone offscreen, gesturing to ask for a cigarette, which, judging from his ensuing disappointment, is denied him. Then he indicates Leopoldo, as if to say there's no point in asking him. And in fact, Leopoldo is now serenely and egotistically lighting up a cigarette for himself.

SPEAKER: And this is Leopoldo. And here's Moraldo, the youngest of us all.

Moraldo, sitting on the metal railing of the terrace, is gazing intently at the sky. Then he turns to his companions.

MORALDO *(offscreen):* Hey, look how pretty it is out here; there's lightning.

At the microphone, Riccardo sings with inspiration as he gazes at the sky.

SPEAKER: And the tenor who's singing is Riccardo. Just as in past years, this is more or less his night.

On a path running between the various pavillions of the Kursaal, Fausto strolls with a girl.

SPEAKER: And here's Fausto, our leader and spiritual guide.

Evidently winding up a long discussion, Fausto turns to stare at the girl with feigned passionate intensity.

FAUSTO: Now do you believe me?

The girl holds his stare tranquilly for some moments. Then, listening to Riccardo's song in the distance, she softly hums the melody and answers Fausto with some annoyance.

GIRL: Come off it, you think I'm stupid or something? Here, give me my shoe.

She takes her shoe from his hand and starts to go back inside. Fausto holds her back and tries to embrace her.

FAUSTO: I'll give it to you, but you give me a kiss!

Increasingly annoyed, the girl tries to free herself.

GIRL: Let me go!

But Fausto continues to pull her to him.

FAUSTO *(insisting):* Come on, give me a kiss.

GIRL. I said let me go!

FAUSTO: And don't put on such a show.

GIRL *(angrily):* Oh let me go, stupid, you big dope. *(She manages to pull herself loose and starts to go off.)* Well! ... Now do you understand?

FAUSTO *(catching her again):* But look, silly, you promised me ...

GIRL: What did I promise you?

FAUSTO: Yes, you said that before you left ... *(He leaves the conclusion unspoken.)*

GIRL *(patting his chin derisively):* Oooh ... Yes, poor little boy, lots of promises get made, think how many you made to Sandra.

FAUSTO *(annoyed):* Oh come on, to Sandra! What's she to me?

GIRL: What? What's she to you? Ha, ha ...

She breaks out into ironical laughter, turns and goes inside.

Kursaal terrace. Night.

Riccardo, at the microphone, reads from a slip of paper:

RICCARDO: Miss Siren of 1953: Miss Sandra Rubini!

The audience breaks out into enthusiastic applause. All eyes turn toward the group of contestants.

Sandra's mother, smiling joyfully and much moved, rises from her own table and goes toward her daughter, who is among the other contestants.

SANDRA'S MOTHER: Oh, my darling girl, you see, angel, you see, and you didn't even want to try out! ...

Leopoldo, Moraldo (Sandra's brother), and Alberto join the rest of the audience in wildly applauding Sandra. Alberto turns to Moraldo and joyfully indicates the mother's delight.

ALBERTO: Look how she's carrying on! Your little sister's won.

MORALDO *(smiling):* Yes.

ALBERTO *(offscreen):* Thatagirl, Sandra!

As the audience continues to applaud enthusiastically, Sandra's mother, excited and proud, accompanies her to the platform.

SANDRA'S MOTHER: Go, darling, go, my angel, go!

She hands Sandra over to Riccardo, who leads her over to the microphone.

RICCARDO *(presenting Sandra to the audience):* Miss Siren of 1953!

(The applause resounds even louder.)

(From the sea, a sudden rumble of thunder.)

A stronger gust of wind lifts a little dust on the deserted dance floor.

Alberto waves to Sandra and continues to applaud frantically.

ALBERTO *(turning to his friends offscreen):* She's overcome ...

The wind's intensity increases. A loud clap of thunder follows a blinding flash of lightning. Undaunted, Riccardo tries to keep the ceremony going.

RICCARDO: Ladies and gentlemen, your attention please! Right this minute, the famous film star, Lilia Randi, who's come from Rome just for this occasion, is pinning the winner's ribbon on Miss Siren of 1953, our own lovely Sandra Rubini.

The audience applauds, but less strongly now. A number of people have risen to observe the sky. The wind is quite high and whips about the decorations, lights, and tablecloths.

On the platform, Lilia Randi has pinned the "Miss Siren" ribbon on Sandra and kisses her on both cheeks. Sandra continues to smile with great emotion.

As the applause dies down, Leopoldo, Moraldo, and Alberto, chilled and concerned about the storm, look about; they pull up their jacket collars.

LEOPOLDO: That's the end of the party.

Riccardo beckons Sandra closer to the microphone.

RICCARDO *(struggling bravely against the wind):* And now say a few words into the mike here to your admirers.

SANDRA *(in a tiny little voice):* I ...

RICCARDO *(kidding):* That's wonderful, wonderful, she said "I"!

Shivering, the actress calls to someone from the platform.

ACTRESS: Tognacci, bring me my coat.

The first drops of rain hit the terrace. The audience begins to get up.

MORALDO *(with childish delight):* Hey, look over there, it's lightning!

The first drops of rain are rapidly transformed into a downpour. Calling and shouting, overturning tables in its haste, the crowd makes for the inside rooms of the Kursaal.

Increasingly frightened, Sandra stammers into the microphone.

SANDRA: I didn't want to try out ...

A lady throws a sweater over Sandra's head to ward off the rain, and pulls her away.

Riccardo, at the microphone, assumes a heroic attitude and calls for calm.

RICCARDO: Take it easy, ladies and gentlemen, it's just a little shower. Don't leave your seats ... *(The audience continues to flee in panic).* The party's still going on. It's just a little cloud ...

He rapidly wraps a scarf around his head and joins the general retreat. Antonio, the waiter, makes his way over to Alberto, who is rapidly downing the last of his drink.

ANTONIO: The check, Mr. Alberto!

ALBERTO *(trying to escape):* Look, everybody's leaving.

ANTONIO *(holding him back):* Sure, but meantime you pay up.

But Alberto runs off under the rain.

Main hall of Kursaal. Night.

The crowd begins to flock into the bare, dusty hall of the Kursaal. In one corner, the dismantled pieces of the wooden carts used for floats in the annual flower parade help intensify the impression of a bleak state of abandon.

Kursaal. Outside. Night.

The members of the band, carrying their instruments, are deserting, too. The rain pours down on the terrace. Antonio and some other waiters attempt to pull the straw umbrellas and wicker chairs out of the rain. Assisted by her mother, Sandra staggers along with the crowd. A lady kisses and congratulates her.

LADY: Congratulations, Sandra dear!

Main hall.

Inside, in the increasingly crowded hall, Leopoldo anxiously asks a member of the jury to introduce him to the starlet.

LEOPOLDO: Introduce me to Lilia Randi!

MEMBER OF JURY: Oh not now, this is no time ...

LEOPOLDO: There she is over there; come on, please, introduce me!

Riccardo discovers a piano inside the hall and, together with the guitarist, tries to save the party by beginning to play.

The Actress is standing near a window; the Secretary tries to protect her from the assault of the autograph-hounds.

YOUNG MAN *(receiving an autograph):* Thanks, Miss Randi.

ACTRESS *(grumpily):* You're welcome, you're welcome.

She turns her back on the crowd. Just then, the member of the jury comes up with Leopoldo and ceremoniously introduces him.

MEMBER OF JURY: Miss Randi, I'd like to introduce one of our most outstanding local personalities: Leopoldo Mannucci, the dramatist.

ACTRESS *(with forced politeness):* I'm very pleased to meet you.

LEOPOLDO *(emotionally):* I'm extremely honored, Miss Randi. I've followed your career in the newspapers ...

MEMBER OF JURY *(apologetically):* He's written a tragedy ... Yes ... it's called ... he's the poet of our theatrical association ...

But the starlet has already turned away.

Riccardo and the guitarist are playing energetically, but their efforts seem only to increase the general confusion.

Moraldo is more and more excited by the storm.

MORALDO *(to Riccardo and the guitarist):* It's just beautiful outside, boys. Looks like the end of the world. It's beautiful.

Kursaal terrace. Night.

Outside, the terrace is completely deserted and swept by gusts of wind and rain.

Kursaal hall. Night.

Jam-packed into the hall, the crowd begins to dance. The two musicians have now been joined by Alberto, who is showing off on the traps in imitation of an American jazz drummer.

Sandra, standing against one wall, receives the compliments and congratulations of her girlfriends and of the other contestants for the title of Miss Siren.

VOICES: Marvelous, Sandra ... You feel pretty good, eh? ... Congratulations, Mrs. Rubini!

Beside her, her mother smiles proudly in triumph. Several of the friends come up to kiss Sandra.

BRUNETTE *(shouting):* Now you'll get into the movies, won't you?!

But an expression of suffering has appeared on Sandra's face, and she seems to be breathing with effort. She leans against the wall and presses a hand to her forehead. A moment later she slips to the floor in a faint. Her mother, who has not noticed, continues to smile and thank the admirers. Then, seeing her daughter out cold on the floor, she screams and bends over her.

SANDRA'S MOTHER: Sandra! Oh my God! Oh my God! *(She rises immediately, terrified, and calls her son.)* Moraldo! Moraldo!

Moraldo turns and calls back in worried surprise.

MORALDO: What is it, Mama?

MOTHER: Come here! Your sister's sick!

Followed by Riccardo, Moraldo makes his way through the crowd.

MORALDO: Excuse me. Excuse me, please.

MOTHER: A doctor! A doctor! Call a doctor!

RICCARDO: What's happened, Ma'am?

MOTHER *(ever more terrified)*: A doctor! A doctor!

Moraldo takes a quick look at his sister and tries to calm down his mother.

MORALDO *(taking Sandra's face in his hands)*: Mama, Mama, take it easy! It's nothing. Mama, calm down. Is there a doctor here, please? Stand back! *(To his mother)* Mama, calm down. It's nothing.

Riccardo tries to push back the crowd which has gathered around the girl.

RICCARDO: Yes, there is. Mancinelli. Mancinelli! Mancinelli! Mancinelli!

Doctor Mancinelli, an elderly, bearded gentleman, pushes his way through the crowd.

MANCINELLI: Here I am! What's happened? Here I am, let me through here. Let me through. Stand back! Out of the way!

Moraldo and Riccardo quickly lift Sandra up and, followed by a crowd of people, carry her into a small adjoining room. The doctor follows, trying to turn back the onlookers.

MANCINELLI: Back! Back, I say! Keep back!

MORALDO: It's nothing! She needs air.

They lay her down on a couch. The doctor takes her pulse. The mother continues to whimper.

MOTHER: Moraldo ... just look at her ...

MORALDO: It's nothing, Mama; calm down, come on ...

Riccardo goes back to the doorway, where the crowd is peering in curiously. His eyes search for someone and he calls:

RICCARDO: Fausto, Fausto! Leopoldo, call Fausto. Tell him to come
here.

A girl repeats Riccardo's summons.

GIRL: Fausto, Fausto! Come here.

The doctor leans over Sandra and listens to her heart as Moraldo continues to comfort his still-frightened mother.

MORALDO: Mama, Mama, calm down, calm down. It's nothing.

MOTHER: What d'you mean nothing; look at her!

Fausto makes his way through the crowd in the main hall but stops at the doorway to the little room and looks inquiringly at Leopoldo, who is already stationed there.

LEOPOLDO: Sandra's fainted; she's sick.

The doctor has completed his examination and stands up, silent.

MOTHER *(anxiously):* Is she better?

She leans over Sandra, who opens her eyes.

SANDRA: Mama!

MOTHER: Darling!

Sandra sees Fausto standing in the doorway. She immediately drops her eyes and suddenly bursts into desperate tears, hiding her face in her hands.

SANDRA *(sobbing):* I want to die, I want to die.

Her mother bends over her and rests her face gently on the girl's hair.

MOTHER: Oh my dear little Sandra, my lovely girl, what are you
saying? You want to die just tonight, when you've just

become Miss Siren? No, darling, don't say such things, not even as a joke! *(Turning to the doctor)* Doctor, what's wrong with her?

Fausto, evidently uncomfortable, watches the scene from the doorway. The mother continues to look uncertainly at the doctor as if to elicit an answer. Moraldo is frowning.

MOTHER: Answer!

The doctor looks gravely into the mother's eyes and then at Moraldo.

MANCINELLI *(clapping his hands):* All right, young folks, everybody out.

At the doctor's words, the mother is struck by a sudden suspicion. She looks first at Moraldo, then at Sandra. Moraldo silently turns to gaze at Fausto.

Fausto, who was about to enter, steps back warily and then makes his way out through the crowd.

Street outside Fausto's home. Night.

The rain continues to pour down heavily in the deserted street. Fausto appears, running along the wall, and enters the gate of his home.

Fausto's home. Pantry. Night.

Fausto closes the door, stamps his feet and shakes the rain from his arms. He crosses the pantry in the dark, opens the door to his room, enters, and slams the door behind him. Fausto's home is modest, almost poor.

Fausto's father's bedroom.

In another room, Fausto's father, a man of about fifty, lifts his head from his work. He is in shirtsleeves and wears an eyeshade. On the table before him are some architectural drawings, a plate with the remains of a very frugal supper, and a bottle of wine. He has obviously been working for several hours.

Fausto's father is about to turn back to his work when he hears a noise coming from his son's room. He rises wearily and starts for the door.

Fausto's room. Night.

Fausto has flung a suitcase on the bed and is rapidly filling it with clothing and personal objects.

The door suddenly opens behind him and his father appears.

FATHER *(sarcastically):* Oh, it's you? Back so soon? Because it's raining ...

Fausto cringes, and, like a thief, tries to hide the suitcase with his body. But the father sees it, and his face grows even grimmer.

FATHER *(suspicious):* What are you up to?

Fausto decides to speak. He is extremely upset, and tries to adopt a tone of strong conviction, which is unusual in his relations with his father.

FAUSTO: Look, Papa ... I have to leave ... I'm leaving now! ... On business ... You remember I told you about that fellow from Milan who might be able to find me a job? ... Well, I've thought it over ... I'm going to work.

FATHER: At this time of night? *(Pauses; then, decisively)* What have you done now?

FAUSTO *(innocently):* Nothing, nothing, I'm going to work. Aren't you pleased?

FATHER: What kind of work?

FAUSTO: It's a company ... They've set up a company ... They're very straight people ... And come to think of it, could you give me five thousand lire for the ticket? As soon as I get there I'll pay you back.

Fausto's father comes up to the young man and seizes him by the shirt.

FATHER: You little hood, what have you done? Eh? What have you done?

FAUSTO *(frightened):* Nothing, nothing, I'm going to work ... Don't you believe me? I'm taking the one o'clock express ...

VOICE OF MORALDO *(from the street):* Fausto!

Silence. Then the doorbell's ring resounds through the house.

Street outside Fausto's house. Night.

Moraldo is standing in front of the door.

Huddled under the eaves of the house across the street are Alberto, Riccardo and Leopoldo. The lock is suddenly buzzed open.

Fausto's room. Night.

Fausto starts to open the door, but the father stops him with a brusque gesture.

FATHER: Stay here. I'll go.

Street outside Fausto's house. Night.

Standing in the rain, Moraldo repeats softly:

MORALDO: Fausto.

But he is surprised to find Fausto's father appearing at the door

Fausto's home. Hallway. Night.

Fausto stands in the doorway of his room. The father and Moraldo are at the front door.

MORALDO *(calmly):* Hello, Mr. Moretti. How are you?

After some moments of silence, the father turns toward Fausto with a suspicious look.

FAUSTO *(to cut him off):* Oh, hi Moraldo! Come on in. Come in, come in. Come on in.

Still smiling with melancholy detachment, Moraldo crosses the hall and enters Fausto's room. in some embarrassment, avoiding his friend's eyes.

Fausto's room. Night.

FAUSTO: Have a seat. *(To his father)* Excuse us, Papa. You know.

After a moment's hesitation, Fausto closes the door and goes back to filling his suitcase, avoiding Moraldo's eyes.

Moraldo leans against the wall, his head lowered.

FAUSTO: That's some downpour. Well, that's the end of the season. Too bad. *(Pauses)* Want a smoke? *(He holds out a package of cigarettes.)* ... Here ...

MORALDO *(not taking the package):* There's only one left.

FAUSTO: No. It doesn't matter. No. I don't want it now.   .

After hesitating briefly, Moraldo takes the cigarette. Fausto is ready with a match.

FAUSTO: This'll last three days at least. Pretty long, isn't it?

He goes back to his suitcase.

MORALDO: So ... you're leaving?

FAUSTO *(affecting nonchalance):* Yes, I'm going away.

MORALDO: You going to be away long?

FAUSTO: I don't know ... it depends ...

Moraldo gazes at his cigarette and finally works up his courage.

MORALDO *(softly):* And Sandra?

FAUSTO *(undaunted):* Sandra! *(With forced gaiety)* She was elected Miss Siren? That was terrific. She must be happy, no?

MORALDO *(quietly):* Sandra's pregnant.

Fausto stands there, tense and horrified. But with histrionic rapidity his face assumes an expression of intense suffering and noble self-sacrifice.

He suddenly turns to face Moraldo.

FAUSTO *(his voice low and vibrant):* Yes, I know. That's why I'm going. Try to understand, Moraldo. I'd like to fix things up ... But how can I?

He looks at Moraldo, as if awaiting an answer. Moraldo is silent, avoiding his eyes.

FAUSTO: I'm out of work just like you are. I haven't a cent to my name, that's why I'm going to Milan. I want to try to get a start. Yes, of course, as soon as I get fixed up, I'll be back. I'll be back right away.

Another strained silence.

FAUSTO: Don't you believe me?

Moraldo gazes at Fausto with his same melancholy smile.

MORALDO: I didn't say anything.

Fausto comes toward Moraldo as if he wishes to speak out, then sighs and goes over to the window, turning his back to his friend.

FAUSTO: Look, Moraldo, we understand one another. I really love Sandra ... I swear to you. I swear by whatever you want. You want me to swear by my mother? I really love her. It was destiny.

He turns slowly and gazes at Moraldo as if alluding to a misfortune which has overtaken someone else. He shakes his head, seeing that Moraldo has not moved.

FAUSTO: Now tell the truth. If you were in my shoes wouldn't you try to get a start first? Wouldn't you?

Moraldo raises his head.

MORALDO: I don't know. Well, then what? Eh?

Fausto goes back to the bed, closes the suitcase and is suddenly struck by an idea. He turns to Moraldo as if to propose a jaunt:

FAUSTO *(his face lighting up):* Moraldo, why don't you come with me?

The proposal astonishes Moraldo. Fausto is more and more taken with his idea.

FAUSTO *(warmly):* That's the thing; come on, we'll go together ... What would you do here this winter, anyway?

MORALDO: Are you crazy?

FAUSTO: It doesn't matter if we don't find work in Milan ... We can try somewhere else ... and we always said we would get out of this place someday.

MORALDO: Right now?

FAUSTO: Believe me, this is just the right time. It's just the right time! And Sandra will be so happy. You'll see. Come on, let's go.

Fausto grabs his suitcase, takes his raincoat and cap from the chair and starts for the door. He is elated; he believes he has solved the whole problem.

FAUSTO: Let's go outside and talk about it. Keep quiet, don't make any noise. Come on. Let's go! Turn out the light.

He opens the door and sees his father standing in the hall, staring at him with a black expression on his face. Fausto tries to smile.

Hall. Night.

FAUSTO: Oh, Papa. Sorry, Moraldo. *(An embarrassed pause. Fausto turns to his father.)* Papa ... can you give me that five thousand?

At these words, the father approaches the young man with a menacing expression. His voice is distorted by wrath.

FATHER: What d'you want, five thousand lire? To do what with? To leave?

FAUSTO: No, Papa.

FATHER: First you get into trouble and then you run.

FAUSTO: But you don't understand.

FATHER: I'll murder you! ...

Fausto tries to open the door, but his father is upon him and lands him a terrific blow.

Fausto staggers back and collapses in a corner of the room, cowering like a child, with his hands hiding his head.

FAUSTO: Papa, please.

FATHER: Stop shouting. Come here, stop shouting.

FAUSTO: What are you going to do? Father!

The father is upon him again, but Fausto slips away and flees to another corner of the room.

FATHER: I swear to you ...

In his now uncontrollable rage, the father overturns chairs, pushes aside the table and finally reaches the trapped Fausto. He is about to slam his son again when Moraldo steps between them and stops the father's hand.

MORALDO: Sir ...

FATHER: Get away! Coward! *(He thrusts Moraldo violently aside and manages to catch Fausto at the front door.)* I swear by your poor mother's dead body that this is the last piece of mischief you'll ever do! That girl's father is a decent man like me! He's slaved his whole life long like me! Like me! To raise his family honorably! But I'll take you to the church. *(Almost weeping)* You'll see, I'll kick you all the way there. You bastard.

A sob racks his chest and he drops his hands. Drying his eyes, he goes down the corridor, at the end of which Fausto's little sister has appeared in her nightgown.

SISTER *(sleepily)*: What's going on, Papa?

FATHER: Nothing. Go back to bed. *(Turning to Fausto, his voice trembling with tears)* And you'll marry her, understand? I'll make sure you marry her!

Moraldo stands against the wall, his head bowed.

In the silence, Fausto opens the front door, looks out and sees Riccardo, Leopoldo and Alberto before him. As if caught red-handed, the three slink a few steps back.

Street outside Fausto's home. Night.

The three friends stare at Fausto in silence. It is obvious that they have overheard everything.

RICCARDO: Hi, Fausto.

Fausto drops his head with a great sigh. Then Alberto starts to laugh: a suffocated giggle which gradually becomes louder, open, and derisive.

FAUSTO: Go ahead, laugh, stupid, my father's crying.

Alberto stumbles away from the others, points to Fausto, doubles over and crumbles against the wall as if dying of laughter.

Church. Inside. Day.

(In the background, Riccardo's song.)

In the organist's box, Riccardo is passionately singing Schubert's "Ave Maria." The notes of the organ and the tenor's voice resound through the great nave of the old medieval church.

SPEAKER: And they did get married. And it was a lovely wedding, even if it was prepared a little hastily. Riccardo sang Schubert's "Ave Maria" and made everybody cry. And the Dean, who knew us from childhood, made a very moving speech.

DEAN *(in a tremulous voice):* Dearest bride and groom, you cannot imagine with what great joy I have just united you in holy matrimony. And you dear Fausto ... and you dear Sandra ...

Riccardo's voice grows louder.

(Organ music grows louder.)

Alberto congratulates Fausto, who is obviously much moved.

ALBERTO: Well? It was unforgettable ... Good boy.

The ceremony is over. The organ plays its last cadenzas at top volume.

The procession has been organized again in great confusion, to the contradictory and amateurish orders of Sandra's father and others.

Fausto and Sandra start forward, smiling and much moved; they are stopped repeatedly by friends and relatives who embrace them.

His eyes shining, sincerely moved, Fausto thanks them all, accepts their embraces and nods repeatedly.

FAUSTO *(moved):* Thanks, thanks everybody ... It was beautiful ... Thanks ... Good, good ...

Fausto's father, in a worn blue suit, follows the couple with Sandra's mother on his arm. He is obviously intimidated. Four or five excited and curious little girls with long white handbags jump about in front of the couple and precede them to the door. Behind them all comes Moraldo, with his usual detached smile; he gazes at the ceiling and the lighted candles ...

A photographer stops the group as it moves toward the door and snaps the ritual photograph.

Railroad station. Outside. Day.

(Train whistle.)

The train starts to pull out. Fausto and Sandra stand at the window of a first-class car; she holds a handkerchief to her eyes and he waves goodbye.

SANDRA *(through her tears):* 'Bye, Mama ...

Two separate groups are gathered on the platform. The first includes the relatives (Sandra's parents and aunts, Fausto's father and his little daughter).

(Goodbyes, ad lib.)

In the second group are Leopoldo, Moraldo, Alberto, Riccardo and Alberto's sister.

They all shout and wave their handkerchiefs until the train is well out of the station. Giudizio, the town fool, chases after the train with his wheelbarrow, shouting gaily. Fausto can be seen looking out the window.

FAUSTO *(shouting):* So long, Papa.

Overcome by emotion, Fausto's father responds with a slight wave of his hand.

Piazza outside the station. Day.

The entire company comes out of the station, with only Moraldo remaining behind on the platform, watching the train with his usual melancholy, absent look.

The piazza outside is deserted and bleak. Two horse-drawn carriages are parked at the beginning of the boulevard.

Some moments of embarrassed hesitation. Then, openly displaying an attitude of superiority toward Fausto's father, who has remained slightly off to one side, Sandra's mother speaks loudly.

SANDRA'S MOTHER *(to her husband):* Well, shall we go?

Sandra's father, obviously embarrassed, turns to Fausto's father.

SANDRA'S FATHER: Well, Mr. Moretti ... We'll say goodbye now ...

Fausto's father comes forward awkwardly and the two men shake hands. The little girl remains behind.

FAUSTO'S FATHER: Thanks, Mr. Rubini ... *(With great effort)* You'll see, Fausto's not a bad boy, really ...

Emotion prevents him from continuing. He smiles. To alleviate the other man's embarrassment, Sandra's father caresses the little girl's hair.

SANDRA'S FATHER: This is your little daughter, your youngest?

FAUSTO'S FATHER *(with a happy, grateful smile):* Yes, she's a fine child ...

Sandra's mother steps in.

SANDRA'S MOTHER *(curtly):* Of course your son will come live in our house, at least until he is able to provide for Sandra some other way ... Good day ...

The group of Vitelloni watches the scene from a short distance away.

ALBERTO: Why does she have to treat him like that?

Sandra's mother starts off, followed by her husband and her relatives, who politely take their leave of Fausto's father.

Fausto's father makes an awkward little bow and remains standing there with his hat in his hand and his daughter by his side. Riccardo leaves the group of Vitelloni who have been watching the painful scene and comes up to him.

RICCARDO *(in his ringing tenor voice):* May we offer you a drink, Mr. Moretti?

After a moment's hesitation, Fausto's father thanks him with a smile.

FAUSTO'S FATHER: No thanks, Riccardo, I'm going home.

He starts off, taking the little girl by the hand. After a few steps, she turns to look back at the four young men. In the distance, Giudizio can be seen running behind his wheelbarrow.

Café. Inside. Night.

Alberto and Riccardo are playing billiards. Leopoldo sits beside the table keeping score. Moraldo leans his chair against the wall, rests his feet on the table, and rocks gently to and fro.

Street. Night.

The four friends walk slowly along, lost in thought. Riccardo kicks an empty tin can.

RICCARDO: Well, whatever you may say about it, he's in Rome and we're still here in this damned hick town. *(He puts on his hat and sings a few notes.)*

CARUSO: What a fine voice he has!

ALBERTO: Voice? Oh, his voice. So what, everybody has a voice. *(To Moraldo)* But look ... didn't you know anything about this business of Fausto and your sister? Because really, if we want to be objective about it ... Fausto's a real bastard ...

Riccardo stops.

RICCARDO: But they make a nice couple. They looked great together.

ALBERTO: What? A nice couple? *(Chuckling)* She's pretty. She's a great-looking girl, but not Fausto. That face of his.

RICCARDO: Come on, he's got a good body, he's tall ...

LEOPOLDO: No, he's not a bastard ... I'd say he was an instinctive type ... ruled by passion ... gimme a light? ... like a beast of the wilds ...

ALBERTO: Oh come off it! He always thinks he's writing some play. Fausto's a filthy-minded wencher ... It would be like one of you making love to my sister! ...

RICCARDO: I'd love to make love to your sister ...

Alberto looks at him and jokingly lashes a punch at him. Riccardo ducks, leaps over to the empty tin can and poises his foot for the kick.

RICCARDO: Ready!

He kicks it over toward Alberto, who immediately jumps, fakes a shot, then kicks it accurately over to Leopoldo. Leopoldo kicks and misses.

RICCARDO: Pass ...

Riccardo runs up and kicks the can far down the road. The noise has barely died away when a prostitute appears at the corner of a side street. Fortyish, short and dumpy, she trudges wearily along, looking somewhat suspiciously at the four young men, who begin to mock her with rather vulgar expressions as they approach. Moraldo objects and tries to induce his companions to leave her alone.

The prostitute insults them right back; she is evidently accustomed to this type of clowning. She takes a drag of her cigarette.

Riccardo has reached the tin can and kicks it again. As the four friends go off singing, the Speaker's voice resumes.

SPEAKER: And now? What else can we find to do? Another day's over, and we can only go back home, just as we do evening after evening.

Alberto's home. Hallway. Night.

Alberto's mother, fully dressed, is waiting up for him. He kisses her goodnight and goes toward his bedroom, glancing into his sister's room as he passes by.

SPEAKER: Alberto knows his mother won't go to bed until he comes in.

Olga is typing. On the table are some ledgers which she has brought home from the office. She returns Alberto's wave; he continues on toward his own room.

Riccardo's bedroom. Night.

Wearing only his pajama pants, Riccardo stands before the mirror, pulling in his belly and thrusting out his chest. He looks somehwat dismayed.

SPEAKER: Just like every other night, Riccardo finds himself getting fat.

Leopoldo's room. Night.

Leopoldo is sitting at his tiny desk.

SPEAKER: As for Leopoldo, after eating the dinner his aunts have left for him in his room, he prepares to continue work on his new drama. He has put on his favorite record, "Fly Through the Night," sits down at his desk, unscrews his fountain pen ...

Leopoldo unscrews his fountain pen. Leopoldo draws a flower on a sheet of paper. Leopoldo gazes at the ceiling ...

SPEAKER: ... draws a triangle ... follows his characters across the ceiling ...

Leopoldo goes over to the window, which overlooks a narrow courtyard. He takes a long pole and taps on the window next door.

LEOPOLDO: Caterina!

The other window opens and a disheveled, sleepy-looking girl appears.

SPEAKER: She's the next-door maid.

LEOPOLDO *(softly):* How are you, Caterina?

MAID: Not good, with this cold weather. How about you?

LEOPOLDO *(softly):* Well ... I'm working.

MAID *(yawning):* What a pretty moon!

LEOPOLDO *(seductively):* Pretty like you!

Flattered, the girl gestures to ward him off.

MAID: Oh ... you liar! Why do you always play the same song?

LEOPOLDO: It inspires me.

Street. Night.

Moraldo is standing in the middle of the street.

SPEAKER: Just like every other night, only Moraldo's left in the deserted streets.

The great church bell breaks the silence of the night. Moraldo, who has taken out his keys and is about to open the gate, stops to listen to the slowly tolling bell. When the last echoes have died away, he hears the whistle of a train. Instead of opening the gate, Moraldo remains lost in thought. He sits down on a bench and looks up at the starry heavens.

MORALDO *(to himself):* Suppose I left, too?

His train of thought is broken by the sprightly steps of someone approaching, whistling as he goes. Moraldo turns and sees a young boy appear from a side street. He wears a workman's overalls and a railwayman's cap. As he notices Moraldo sitting in the shadows, the boy stops short, as if afraid.

MORALDO *(smiling pleasantly at him):* Hi! Still up at this hour? It's three a.m. Aren't you going to bed?

The boy comes up to Moraldo, smiling. Under the soiled visor of his cap, his funny little face is cheerful and gay.

BOY: I just got up. I always get up at three, every morning.

MORALDO *(surprised and serious):* Where are you going?

BOY: I work at the station.

Moraldo is much struck by this, and reacts with an odd little laugh. Then he reaches out and rumples the boy's hair.

MORALDO: What d'you mean, work?

BOY: I work at the station.

MORALDO: Well ... come here, sit down. What do you do? What kind of work do you do?

BOY: I told you, I work.

MORALDO *(taking his cap):* And this is a railwayman's cap.

BOY: Yes.

MORALDO: Well ... tell me, are you happy?

BOY *(shrugging his shoulders):* Oh, it's pretty good ...

MORALDO: Want a cigarette?

BOY *(nodding):* Sure ...

Moraldo searches through his pockets but is obviously embarrassed not to find any cigarettes.

MORALDO: I'm sorry. They're all gone.

As if to relieve Moraldo's embarrassment, the boy backs away to continue on his way.

BOY: That's all right ... 'Bye ...

MORALDO: Listen ...

The boy goes down the center of the street with his cheerful step.

BOY: So long.

MORALDO: So long.

Courtyard. Day.

A little old man with slightly looney eyes and a baseball cap on his head is tinkering with a complicated apparatus equipped with wings and propellors.

Alberto enters the courtyard, comes by the little man and inspects the apparatus with the air of an expert.

ALBERTO: Hello, sir. How's the flight capsule coming along?

INVENTOR *(reserved and slightly diffident):* It's coming along, it's coming along ...

He checks the motion of a propellor with some anxiety.

ALBERTO: And when will we be flying?

INVENTOR *(significantly):* Sooner than my enemies think.

ALBERTO *(going off):* Good luck, sir!

Alberto comes up to a barred window, through which we see an office whose shelves are filled with files. At a table near the window, Olga is checking accounts at the adding machine.

ALBERTO *(softly):* Olga! Olga!

Olga turns, removes her glasses and looks gravely at her brother.

ALBERTO *(softly):* Is the boss there?

OLGA *(without considering this last question):* What d'you want?

ALBERTO: Listen, Olga? You have to do me a favor ... then on Sunday I have a deal coming off and I'll pay you back ... *(He raises one finger, affectedly.)* Lend me a thousand lire?

Olga stares at him at length. She is obviously exhausted.

ALBERTO *(admiringly, with feigned concern):* You worked all night long, eh? *(Softly)* But I'm going to tell that guy off, you know? He should raise your salary!

Olga opens her bag and takes out a bill.

OLGA: I can only give you five hundred.

(A whistle.)

RICCARDO'S VOICE: Alberto!

Alberto turns toward the courtyard entrance, where he sees Riccardo waving wildly at him. Then he takes the money from Olga.

ALBERTO: Thanks, Olga, thanks a lot.

He smiles at her and waves goodbye, then joins the greatly excited Riccardo.

RICCARDO: Listen, Massimo and Leopoldo are going to Bologna. The trotting races are on.

ALBERTO: So?

RICCARDO: They've given me a sure winner; why don't we put something on him too? A thousand lire'd be enough. I have three hundred. What about you?

Olga, who has overheard the conversation, shakes her head and goes back to work.

Beach. Day.

A windy, gray day. Long white-crested waves rake the sea. The beach is deserted.

SPEAKER: By now the seaside is deserted, even on Sundays.

Bundled up in overcoats and hats, Alberto, Riccardo, Leopoldo and Moraldo stand at the water's edge contemplating the sea, close enough to have to step back now and then when a longer wave threatens to wet their feet. No one speaks. Each is absorbed in following his own thoughts. Finally Riccardo breaks the long silence.

RICCARDO: Suppose somebody came along and offered you ten thousand lire, would you go in swimming?

LEOPOLDO *(tonelessly, shivering):* Huh? ...

The wind smashes the crests of the waves. The four young men start strolling along the shore in Indian file.

(A dog barks.)

A German shepherd races toward them from a group of shacks not far off. Alberto greets the joyously barking dog with equal gaiety.

ALBERTO: Hey there, dog!

The dog stops for a moment, then heads straight for Alberto. Riccardo picks up a piece of driftwood and tosses it to Alberto, who then throws it some distance behind the dog. The dog turns back to pick up the stick as Alberto runs toward him. Alberto tosses the stick a second time, again in the direction of the shacks, and the dog continues to play.

The other three friends have slowed their pace.

LEOPOLDO *(indicating Alberto):* I don't know ... He always wants to fool around like that ...

Fifty yards ahead, Alberto and the dog continue their game. By now they are quite close to the shacks. The dog races toward the shacks with the stick in his teeth, ignoring Alberto's calls.

Running breathlessly after the dog, Alberto sees a man and a woman standing near the shacks talking. Parked on the road behind them is a medium-sized Fiat.

ALBERTO: Dog!

The couple turns. The woman is Olga.

The dog runs to bring the stick to the man with her. Astonished and perturbed, Alberto cannot decide whether to go on or turn back. He looks from his sister to her companion. The couple has not stirred.

A long pause, interrupted only by the barking of the dog, which wags its tail happily at its master's feet.

At last Alberto turns to go back. Olga moves.

OLGA *(calling softly):* Alberto!

Alberto stops but does not turn toward her. Olga comes up to him.

OLGA *(pleading, but firmly):* You mustn't tell Mama you saw me.

Alberto does not look at her; he answers with rancor and scorn.

ALBERTO: You said it was all over!

Olga tries to hold him back, placing her hand on his arm. Alberto shakes her off.

ALBERTO: Leave me alone! ...

He starts toward the water. Moraldo, Riccardo, and Leopoldo come up, slowing down and stopping to gaze at Olga and the man with her.

Dissimulating their dismay, Moraldo, Riccardo, and Leopoldo turn back toward the pier, followed by Alberto. To break the painful silence, Riccardo can think of nothing better than stopping to pick something up from the sand.

RICCARDO: Hey, look what a pretty shell!

Alberto has turned to look toward the road, where the car is rapidly driving off ...

Olga's room. Night.

Olga is at her desk typing. She turns to look toward the door.

(Sound of a door closing.)

The bedroom door opens and Alberto appears, very tense.

OLGA *(surprised):* Hi, Alberto, we seem to be meeting all day long.

ALBERTO: Look. I don't want to be made a fool of by my friends because of you.

OLGA *(tense):* Oh, so your friends ... allow themselves the luxury of laughing at other people ...

ALBERTO *(angrily):* Yes! *(Softly)* You've got to stop it with that guy. *(Scornfully)* What can you hope for from him?

OLGA *(simply):* Nothing. I don't want to hope for anything.

ALBERTO *(emphasizing each syllable):* He's a married man.

OLGA: Don't shout, Mama's sleeping.

ALBERTO: He's got a wife. He's married.

OLGA: I know. But they don't live together.

ALBERTO *(sarcastically):* So what? Can he marry you? *(Pauses)* Can he marry you?

OLGA *(harshly):* Don't put your nose in my business, Alberto. I've always gotten along all right by myself. I know what I have to do ...

ALBERTO: Oh, you think that just because you work you can do whatever you want to?

OLGA *(firmly):* Yes.

ALBERTO *(getting up):* No! I say no. You're my sister! *(He comes over to her, shaking his finger under her nose.)* And you make Mama cry ...

OLGA: Get your hands down. *(Staring fixedly at him)* Get out of here, Alberto. Get out!

ALBERTO: If you make Mama cry ...

He slams the door behind him as he leaves.

Café. Outside. Day.

A warm October day. Leopoldo, Riccardo, Alberto, and Moraldo are sitting in their overcoats outside the café.

SPEAKER: And one fine day, when we'd almost forgotten all about him ...

Caruso comes up the boulevard.

CARUSO *(shouting):* Hey you guys, Fausto's back!

The news registers first on Riccardo.

RICCARDO *(brightening):* Fausto's back!

CARUSO *(nearer now):* Yes, yes. He's got a moustache!

RICCARDO: Where is he?

CARUSO: Back there!

MORALDO *(shouting):* Fausto?

The four friends scramble from their seats and run toward Fausto and Sandra, who have now come in sight and are waving and calling as they approach.

FAUSTO *(shouting):* Hey, boys!

RICCARDO: Fausto!

The two groups meet in the middle of the street. Sandra remains slightly behind her husband; she is wearing the same dress, with a little veiled hat, which she wore the day she left for her honeymoon.

Fausto embraces Riccardo and Leopoldo, clapping them on the shoulders.

FAUSTO: We've been looking for you for an hour!

RICCARDO: You look great with a moustache!

LEOPOLDO: Yes! You look great. Bravo!

RICCARDO: Tomorrow I'll start one too!

FAUSTO *(embracing Alberto affectionately):* Hi, Alberto, we've been looking for you for an hour! *(Fausto is carrying a portable phonograph. He goes toward the café tables.)* Hey, I've got something really terrific here. Come and see.

ALBERTO: What have you brought? A cake?

Surrounded by the friends, and answering their questions about the trip, Fausto puts the phonograph on the table, opens the case, and puts on a record.

FAUSTO: We saw Wanda Osiris, you know?

SANDRA: It was just marvelous ...

FAUSTO: Yes, it was beautiful. Not bad. It was a good show, but not all that great ...

SANDRA: She came down a long, long stairway ...

Alberto jokingly sings a few lines from one of Osiris' famous songs.

FAUSTO: Quiet down, quiet down, now listen to this mambo ... Listen ... *(The music begins.)* There was a dancer ... the best part was this: there was this dancer that was dancing like this ...

Following the rhythm of the mambo, Fausto begins to dance by himself, with affectedly elegant movements. As the others watch, he moves from the sidewalk into the street. Alberto gets up and comes closer to observe his steps.

ALBERTO: Listen, Fausto, will you teach it to me later?

FAUSTO *(continuing to dance):* Sure, it's easy.

Now Alberto begins to dance too, awkwardly trying to imitate his friend, as the others look on from the café tables.

Moraldo turns to look at Sandra, who is keeping time to the mambo. He smiles at her.

SANDRA: Nice, isn't it?

MORALDO *(hanging an arm around her neck):* Are you happy?

SANDRA *(half-closing her eyes):* Yes, so happy ...

In the middle of the street, Fausto and Alberto continue their dance number.

Religious articles shop. Inside Day.

SPEAKER: And everything would have gone on just as it always had if Fausto's father-in-law hadn't gotten a strange idea.

A huge old-fashioned shop with walnut counters and shelves in white and gold. The shop is full of statues, statuettes, decorated candles, religious books, etc. As the street door opens, a tinkling carillon chimes.

Behind the counter, a cordial and energetic-looking man of about forty-five (Michele) is showing some rosaries to two silent nuns.

MICHELE *(joyfully):* Here's our friend Rubini! Just a moment, I'll be right with you!

SANDRA'S FATHER: Take your time, take your time, Michele. *(Softly, to Fausto)* What a good churchy smell in here, eh?

Fausto, who had been sniffing it, nods respectfully but without enthusiasm. He looks around at the ecstatic faces of the papier-mâché and plaster saints.

SANDRA'S FATHER *(still speaking softly):* No, you'll see, this will suit you just fine. *(Then, somewhat embarrassed, he gazes at Fausto's suit.)* Maybe you'd better buy a clerk's smock.

Fausto frowns but does not answer.

Meanwhile, Michele has finished with the two nuns, who go out, passing between Fausto and Mr. Rubini; their heads are bowed and they mumble a scarcely intelligible farewell.

(Carillon.)

MICHELE *(sincerely cordial):* So here you are ... my dear friend! *(He embraces Rubini.)* And this young man is your son-in-law? Eh? *(He shakes Fausto's hand vigorously.)* I'm very pleased to meet you ... my congratulations ... a little late, but most sincere. You're a very lucky fellow! *(Significantly)* Very! What's doing in Rome? Rubini said you honeymooned in Rome, no? *(Pause)* Well ... I'll tell you right off ... What's your name?

FAUSTO: Fausto Moretti.

MICHELE: Well, Fausto, I'll tell you right off: As you see, all of my business is right here ... it's fairly small ...

SANDRA'S FATHER *(intensely admiring):* You call it small! ...

MICHELE: We built it up by ourselves ... Frankly, Fausto, I really need a boy, or a handyman ... You know, to load and unload stuff, open and close the store ... But I've preferred to do it this way. I prefer to take you on.

SANDRA'S FATHER: Fausto, thank the gentleman ...

FAUSTO: Thanks.

MICHELE: Not at all! I'm happy to be able to help a young man who's just getting started in life ... Anyway, you must feel perfectly at home here. Agreed? *(Shakes Fausto's hand.)* When shall we start?

SANDRA'S FATHER: Right away, if you like!

FAUSTO *(surprised and reluctant):* Right away?

SANDRA'S FATHER: That way you can get an idea ... You can see ...

Michele's wife, Giulia, enters through the arch dividing the store from the back rooms; she is carrying some papers.

MICHELE: Oh, Giulia, come here ...

SANDRA'S FATHER: Good afternoon ...

MICHELE: ... You know Mr. Rubini ... This is Sandra's husband ... who'll be helping us from now on.

Giulia is a serious, slightly faded-looking woman of about forty-five. She bows her head as she normally does with the religious customers, and murmurs a greeting.

GIULIA: Pleased to meet you. *(To her husband)* The truck's here ...

MICHELE: Be right there!

SANDRA'S FATHER: Something else ... Should he buy a smock?

MICHELE: For today he can wear this one.

He opens a cabinet, takes out a long gray smock and hands it to Fausto, who, with the aid of the two men, puts it on with some distaste, wrinkling his nose.

MICHELE *(solemnly):* There you are! You're on the job. *(Smiling)*

Now, Fausto, go out in the courtyard and supervise the unloading. Here's the shipping list. *(He takes the forms from Giulia and hands them to Fausto.)* And be sure to keep a sharp eye on the men; they break everything. It's very fragile stuff. Go on, go on.

Giulia has started for the back room. After a moment's hesitation, Fausto slowly follows her. At the arch, he looks back in some anguish at his father-in-law, who is standing at the door with Michele. Sandra's father returns Fausto's gaze wordlessly. Fausto waves weakly and disappears into the back room.

Sandra's father and Michele remain alone.

Store. Day.

Toward evening. The first shadows begin to invade the store.

Michele, Fausto, and Giulia are sitting motionless in the gathering dusk, each behind his own counter.

(Bells toll.)

Fausto steals glances at Michele and at Giulia. His expression is somewhere between boredom and the diffidence that his new surroundings inspire in him.

A long silence. Fausto cocks his ears: among the voices of the passers-by on the sidewalk outside, he seems to recognize someone's.

At that moment, he sees Alberto, Riccardo, Leopoldo, and Moraldo through the glass door. They are walking by slowly, feigning nonchalance and purposely avoiding looking inside the store.

The four friends disappear for a moment and reappear at the large window, where they pretend to be interested in the statues on display there. Their comments can be heard only dimly from inside. They are making an obvious effort not to look at Fausto, in order not to burst out laughing.

Michele's attention is aroused and he looks curiously at these four odd surveyors of his wares. Giulia, too, looks up from her sewing. Michele switches on the window lights, and the four young men respond with a lengthy, childish "Oh!" Michele turns to look at them, then switches on the center chandelier, flooding the store with violent light.

Store. Outside.

As the inside lights go on, the four friends emit another, even lengthier "Oh!" Now they can clearly see Fausto, who is imprisoned behind the counter like an animal in a cage. Alberto and Riccardo begin to grimace at each other.

ALBERTO *(indicating Fausto):* What a worker!

RICCARDO: Let's go in! We'll pretend to be customers; come on! Come on! ...

Amused by the idea, Leopoldo laughs too.

MORALDO: Cut it out; let's go away.

ALBERTO: Let me be.

MORALDO: But you'll make him lose his job. *(He starts to walk away, turning to repeat to the other three.)* Leave him alone!

Alberto is the last to leave, after pretending to examine a statue with the eye of an art connoisseur.

Further along the same street.

Sandra wanders idly up and down the crowded street. She walks gracefully, with the proud, happy air of a young bride.

Someone suddenly calls her, and two girls hurry up behind.

FIRST GIRL: Sandra! You look fine! When did you get back?

The girls speak in tones of feigned cordiality. Obviously they are bent on humiliating her.

SECOND GIRL: How does it feel to be called "Mrs."?

SANDRA *(proudly):* Fausto's got a job.

FIRST GIRL *(amazed):* Ah, he's working?

SANDRA: I'm going to pick him up now.

SECOND GIRL: You're right to keep an eye on him ... you know?

The two friends laugh together.

FIRST GIRL: No ... Why? Fausto's a good boy! Maybe a little bit fickle! ... You must love it in your little house!

SANDRA *(simply):* No, for now we're still at my mother's.

SECOND GIRL: Oh, of course! You didn't have time ... It was all so sudden ...

The eyes of the two friends stray quite openly toward Sandra's belly.

FIRST GIRL *(softly):* You know, you can't see a thing, not a thing. *(Sandra turns pale and the friend twists the knife.)* Have you still got a long time?

SANDRA *(lowering her eyes, wounded):* I'm sorry, I really have to go. So long.

GIRLS: So long, Sandra. Good luck! Regards to Fausto! Let's get together sometime!

Sandra goes off through the crowd, walking rapidly along the sidewalk. Her humiliated and offended expression changes when she sees Fausto in front of the store, pulling down the iron screen protecting the display window.

Her face lights up. Joyful and moved, she runs across the street toward him.

SANDRA: Fausto!

FAUSTO: Hi, Sandra!

SANDRA: Fausto! I've come to pick you up.

Fausto smiles joyfully, like a child who sees his mother coming to pick him up after the first day at school.

He takes her in his arms and kisses her on the lips.

SANDRA *(modest, but happy):* We're in public!

FAUSTO: You're my wife! *(Proudly)* You know, I sold a statue this high!

SANDRA *(admiringly, happy):* Really?

FAUSTO: Yes I did.

SANDRA *(tenderly moved):* You're wonderful.

FAUSTO: And you know what we'll do now? We'll go to the movies. Me and you.

SANDRA: Wonderful.

FAUSTO: Do we have enough money?

SANDRA: Yes, yes, look, I've got some.

FAUSTO: That's my smart girl.

Sandra nods and winks her eye craftily, with pathetic complicity.

Movie theater. Inside.

An usherette leads Fausto and Sandra to seats in the crowded, smoke-filled orchestra, as intermission advertisement slides are flashed onto the screen.

FAUSTO *(tenderly protective):* Is this all right for you? Can you see?

SANDRA *(nodding):* Look at that beautiful refrigerator.

FAUSTO: Pretty soon we'll get one too.

An advertisement for powdered milk appears on the screen, showing an adorable infant.

SANDRA *(touched):* How cute! *(Fausto searches through his pockets.)* Are you looking for a cigarette?

FAUSTO: Yes.

She opens her handbag and takes out a package of cigarettes, which she displays to Fausto with pride.

FAUSTO *(touched):* Thanks. I've got the matches.

SANDRA *(more intimately):* You know, Papa really likes you? And you know what Mama told me this morning? I was in the bedroom and she said, "Sandra, come here a minute." So I went, and she said that Papa wants to build on a wing for us. But for now we can't let on that we know anything about it...

Meanwhile Fausto has lit Sandra's cigarette and his own. He is about to toss away the match when the beautiful woman sitting beside him holds her own unlit cigarette out to him.

LADY *(in a low-pitched, silken voice):* Would you please give me a light?

Fausto quickly holds out the match. The woman leans over and slowly lights her cigarette.

LADY *(not looking at Fausto):* Thanks.

FAUSTO: Not at all.

Much struck by her, Fausto hides his inner turmoil by staring at the screen. The light music accompanying the advertisements ceases, to be followed a few moments later by the dramatic music introducing the main film.

(Dramatic music.)

Fausto turns to Sandra, who has whispered something to him.

FAUSTO: What?

SANDRA *(softly):* That way we can all live together, can't we?

FAUSTO *(distracted):* Of course.

But it is obvious that his thoughts are elsewhere. He pretends to watch the screen as Sandra cuddles up against him, but he is actually watching his beautiful neighbor out of the corner of his eye.

The beautiful neighbor is watching Fausto too out of the corner of her eye. When their eyes meet, they immediately snap them back to the screen.

(Dramatic music.)

Sandra's head rests on Fausto's shoulder as she attentively follows the story unfolding on the screen. The actors' voices are heard.

VOICE OF ACTOR: Don't believe it, darling, please.

VOICE OF ACTRESS *(whispering):* Oh yes. I should trust you, then.

VOICE OF ACTOR: I've always been suspicious of that lawyer. Bill told me ...

The beautiful woman, apparently impassive, watches the screen as Fausto slowly moves his knee toward hers.

The two knees touch; after a few moments, the woman shifts her position slightly, drawing her knee away.

Fausto leans over to kiss Sandra's hair.

FAUSTO *(indicating the actors on the screen):* Great, aren't they?

SANDRA: Yes, really great.

She smiles happily, leans her cheek ever more firmly on her husband's shoulder and turns her undivided attention back to the film.

Fausto has reached the lady's knee once again. He remains still for a moment, then turns to look her in the face.

The beautiful woman is still watching the screen, but her mysterious, exciting smile is even more intense now.

After a few moments she bends toward Fausto to look at her wristwatch. Then, with a sigh, she rises and starts for the exit.

Fausto holds his breath; his eyes follow her as she walks up the aisle; he fidgets excitedly on his seat and then turns to Sandra.

FAUSTO: Sandra, listen.

SANDRA *(turning in astonishment):* What?

FAUSTO *(softly):* I'll be right back ... Hold my seat.

SANDRA *(alarmed):* Don't you feel well?

FAUSTO *(quickly):* No. No. I feel fine ... I'll be right back ...

He gets up, stumbles over the feet of the other people in his row and hurries toward the exit.

Movie theater. Outside. Night.

The beautiful lady wraps her fur tightly about her neck, leaves the theater and starts along the semi-deserted street. She hears footsteps behind her but does not turn.

Fausto appears at the theater doors. He looks about in hesitation.

The lady has turned the corner and disappeared.

A street. Night.

Breathless from running and from emotion, Fausto catches up with her.

FAUSTO: Ma'am, Ma'am. Excuse me.

The lady does not answer. She walks on, eyes straight ahead.

An alley. Night.

She turns into a dimly lit, tranquil little street, stops in front of the great doorway of an old building and puts her key in the lock.

Fausto catches up with her once more and stops her.

FAUSTO *(panting):* Good evening, Ma'am. When can I see you? Because now ...

The woman stares at him in innocent amazement.

LADY: What do you want anyway?

FAUSTO *(insisting):* Give me your phone number.

LADY *(pretending to take offense):* What d'you mean, telephone? Go away.

FAUSTO: No, wait a minute. Don't close the door, Look ...

The lady steps inside. Fausto resolutely puts his foot in the door and forces his way into the dark entranceway.

FAUSTO: I have to tell you something ...

Entranceway, old building. Night.

He throws his arms about her and kisses her. The lady does not resist, but assumes an air of astonishment. Fausto kisses her again, on the mouth.

LADY *(extracting herself from his embrace):* What are you doing? Are you mad?

FAUSTO *(in a strangled voice):* I know you, I know you. This summer you wore a white bathing suit. Don't you remember, at the Kursaal?

LADY: So? ... I know you, too. You were with someone, I believe, at the movies. Some pretty girl ...

FAUSTO: Me? No. *(Insisting)* When can we see each other?

LADY *(alarmed):* Go away. What are you thinking of, I'm a married woman. My maid's upstairs.

Fausto kisses her again.

FAUSTO: Then tell me when ... tomorrow night!

LADY *(softly, with effort):* Never. Never again.

FAUSTO: Day after tomorrow? Yes?

LADY: No.

FAUSTO: Then when?

LADY: When we happen to meet. *(Then, rapidly)* Let's leave it to fate. Goodbye!

The lady starts up the stairs. Fausto follows.

FAUSTO: No, wait a minute, don't go away. I have to tell you something important. Come back here. Listen.

She has disappeared up the stairs.

LADY: Go away!

Fausto remains alone. He passes his hand mechanically over his hair, then straightens his tie and smiles in conceited self-satisfaction.

Street. Night.

Out in the street again, Fausto gazes up at the windows of the building with the same pleased expression. Then he walks off, and suddenly breaks into a run.

Movie theater. Outside. Night.

Outside the theater, Sandra looks about, alone and bewildered. The neon signs and the lights of the cafés have already been turned off.

A theater employee is plastering "Today" signs on the photographs of the next day's show. Fausto suddenly comes into the piazza at a run, and after a moment's hesitation, heads toward Sandra, calling to her with feigned, aggressive surprise.

SANDRA: Fausto!

FAUSTO: Sandra! Are you here?

Sandra gazes at him in anguish.

SANDRA: Where were you?

FAUSTO *(improvising badly)*: I saw a fellow ... I forgot I'd said I'd meet him ... but I was late ... *(Then, as if wishing to reenter the theater)* Is it all over? *(He takes Sandra's arm and leads her away.)* That's too bad! How did it end? *(Profoundly disturbed, Sandra allows him to lead her away.)* Does she die?

SANDRA *(her voice trembling):* No ... They get married.

Two tears roll down her cheeks.

FAUSTO *(conversationally):* She's a good actress. Do you remember her in that other picture we saw in Rome? ... *(He stops short.)* Sandra! What's the matter? Are you crying?

Sandra shakes her head, tries to smile, and wipes a tear from the corner of her eye.

SANDRA: No, no.

FAUSTO: Yes, you are, you're crying! What's the matter? *(Pause)* What have I done?

Sandra yields to her emotions: She leans against Fausto, her head bowed.

SANDRA *(in a choked voice):* I'm afraid ...

FAUSTO *(truly surprised):* Afraid? Of what?

SANDRA: I don't know ... I'm afraid. *(Ashamed, she tries to hide her tears with nervous laughter; she walks a few steps further on, takes out a handkerchief and blows her nose.)* I'm sorry ...

Fausto is profoundly disturbed and ashamed of himself; at the sight of his wife, so small and defenseless in the deserted street, he is overcome with tenderness. He, too, has an impulse to weep, and speaks in a tone of childish sadness.

FAUSTO: No, Sandra, don't be like that ...

He comes up to her, takes her hand and kisses it.

Now Sandra feels a rush of maternal pity.

SANDRA *(reassuring and tender):* No, no ... It's all over, darling. If you stay beside me, I'm not afraid ...

FAUSTO *(touched, sincere):* But I'll always be beside you ...

Sandra smiles at him through her tears, dries her eyes and takes Fausto's arm.

SANDRA *(smiling):* Let's go home ...

FAUSTO: Yes, let's go back to our little home.

Still trembling with emotion, Fausto walks off down the deserted street with his little bride.

Barbershop. Inside. Day.

Riccardo stands at the mirror trimming his moustache.

SPEAKER: In the next few months, the most important things that happened were that Riccardo grew a moustache ... and Alberto grew sideburns.

Seated nearby, Alberto checks the length of his sideburns in the mirror.

Religious articles shop. Day.

SPEAKER: While Fausto shaved his moustache off.

The store is empty except for Fausto, who is sitting behind the counter gazing at the display window.

SPEAKER: Sometimes his father and his little sister would pass by the store to see him working ...

Fausto's father and sister stop for a moment in front of the window, with the respectful air of those who do not wish to disturb.

Leopoldo's room. Night.

SPEAKER: And Leopoldo too, working as usual ... grew a beard ...

Leopoldo is at the window talking to the maid next door.

MAID *(stifling a yawn and a giggle):* You scare me ...

LEOPOLDO *(softly):* What d'you mean, I thought you liked it.

Main street. Day.

(Trumpets and peasant bagpipes.)

A gray, rainy day. A rather shabby-looking costume parade has begun its procession along the main street of the town.

SPEAKER: And at last, eagerly awaited as always, came Carnival.

Colored banners and paper decorations line the street, swinging gently above the electric lines.

Several horse-drawn carriages filled with costumed girls tossing out streamers and confetti wind their way down the street, accompanied by the cheers and applause of the spectators.

Children masquerading as eighteenth-century Pierrots and damsels promenade with their parents.

Numerous umbrellas have been opened against the drizzling rain. The gayest of all are the poor children, who have simply turned their jackets inside-out and blacked their faces; they race up and down, bump into people, and search for cigarette butts.

Alberto's room. Day.

(Sound of a sewing machine.)

Riccardo, dressed as a musketeer in a plumed hat, gloves, and rapier, is watching the parade from the window. He turns, with the sad, somewhat silly look of one who has been adorned in his costume for a couple of hours already.

RICCARDO *(with forced optimism):* Carnival will be better this year. The people are more anxious to have a good time. Put a mole on the other side too.

ALBERTO: No, one's enough.

Leopoldo, disguised as a Chinese mandarin, sits on Alberto's bed smoking. He nods his approval of Riccardo's words.

Alberto is putting the finishing touches on his make-up at the wardrobe mirror. He is wearing an undershirt and a woman's skirt.

ALBERTO: The dress is ready.

In the next room a woman can be seen working at the sewing machine; this is Elvira, a woman in her mid-forties. She gets up and comes into the bedroom carrying a lace blouse.

ELVIRA *(to Alberto):* Here you are. Now let me alone, or your mother'll be after me. I have to finish the sheets.

ALBERTO: But not like this. They have to be bigger. Like a woman's.

Seeing Alberto's make-up, she shakes her head in disdain.

ELVIRA: Just look at you! I can't stand to look at you like that! ... A handsome fellow like you ...

Riccardo decides to have some fun behind Elvira's back.

RICCARDO *(winking to the others):* She likes him, doesn't she?

Elvira shoots a severe glance at Riccardo and goes out.

RICCARDO *(softly):* Alberto ... *(Gesturing toward Elvira)* She's in love with you.

Leopoldo nods in agreement from the bed. Alberto smiles.

ALBERTO *(very softly):* Yes, yes, even Mama's noticed it! ...

LEOPOLDO *(softly):* Is it true she's loaded?

ALBERTO *(speaking normally):* Why? You want to marry her? *(Shouting)* Elvira. Elvira. The hat! the hat!

So saying, Alberto goes to the door of the dining room, where Elvira has resumed her work in a sea of white linens.

ELVIRA: I certainly don't have your hat.

ALBERTO : You don't? Who does? *(To Leopoldo, handing him the costume)* Hold this! Mama!

He crosses back through the bedroom and goes out the second door into the hall, calling loudly.

Olga's and Mother's bedroom.

A modest room with two beds. Alberto's mother and sister, who have evidently been having an argument, suddenly hush as the young man appears.

The mother rapidly wipes her eyes and goes to the window with her back to Alberto.

Olga remains seated at the foot of her bed and nervously takes a pack of cigarettes from her handbag.

ALBERTO *(to Olga, surprised):* Oh, are you still here? I'm ready, I'm going to go now.

OLGA *(lighting a cigarette):* I'm not going to the dance.

After a moment's hesitation, Alberto shrugs his shoulders with apparent indifference.

ALBERTO: All right, then give me your hat.

OLGA *(annoyed and scornful):* Can't I wear my own hat?

ALBERTO *(disconcerted):* But what am I supposed to do?

Olga gives him an icy stare.

The mother is still at the window, looking at the rain streaking the panes.

ALBERTO *(bitterly):* It must be fate. For once a person can have a little fun, and nobody'll give them a hand.

Without turning, the mother answers in a voice she attempts to make firm and indifferent.

MOTHER: Look in the trunk ... You'll find something there, but don't mess everything up.

Puzzled, Alberto looks at his sister again; she returns his gaze with a slightly scornful expression.

ALBERTO: What's going on here? What are you up to? You're crying, and you're ... *(He approaches his mother.)* Mama, what's the matter?

MOTHER: Nothing. A little headache.

Alberto hesitates, then turns and goes toward the door. As he leaves, he threatens his sister.

ALBERTO: You and I are heading for trouble, you know!

Dining room.

Alberto stamps into the room in an evil temper. Riccardo, who has opened a large chest, calls him over.

RICCARDO: Alberto. Come and have a look. This chest is full of stuff.

ELVIRA: Don't look in there or your mother'll have a fit.

LEOPOLDO *(trying out a dance step):* Riccardo. I really think this is the basic step. Look here!

RICCARDO *(bending down to pick up a photograph):* Who's this character?

Alberto looks at the photo, kisses it and answers simply:

ALBERTO: This is my poor father.

RICCÀRDO *(to Leopoldo):* Leopoldo! Come see this picture. *(Snickers.)*

ALBERTO *(with a shriek of joy):* Here's a hat! Look what I've found!

He extracts an ancient plumed hat from the chest, puts it on and strikes a monstrous pose.

Bertucci Hall. Inside.

A ten-man jazz band is playing a lively mambo on the stage of the theater.

(Music.)

The floor is crowded with masked couples dancing in an atmosphere of tropical abandon. Bunting and paper streamers cascade from the balcony and are pulled down onto the floor by the dancers.

Among the couples are Riccardo and a girl dressed as an oriental slave. Riccardo hums along with the music.

Another couple consists of Alberto, disguised as a woman, and Caruso.

The Rubini family enters one of the boxes. Mrs. Rubini wears an old evening gown; Mr. Rubini is in a blue suit. Sandra, wearing an evening gown and a silver mask, presses tightly against Fausto, who has donned a tuxedo. He watches the frenetic activity on the dance floor with feigned boredom, while Sandra is radiantly enchanted by it.

SANDRA *(to Fausto):* Shall we dance?

Fausto smiles at Sandra and leads her out to the dance floor. Instead of executing the complicated steps that the music calls for, they sway slowly back and forth, check to cheek.

Sandra's expression is of tender and impassioned felicity. With a smile of self-satisfaction on his lips, Fausto keeps to the edge of the floor in order to avoid being bumped into by the other couples. This seems to him more "distinguished." Sandra, ever more tender, half-closes her eyes and hums the melody.

Riccardo, dancing with his slave girl, gives her a vigorous squeeze.

RICCARDO: Did you ever see the basement of this place?

The girl gazes at him with an ironical smile, having understood what Riccardo is aiming at.

Not far off, Leopoldo, in his mandarin outfit, dances with a girl who is also dressed in Chinese costume; she is one of the two girls whom Sandra met on the street.

LEOPOLDO: You had the same idea ... China ... You know what this means for us?

Distracted, the girl does not answer.

LEOPOLDO *(insisting):* It means we have the same kind of sensitivity.

GIRL *(plaintive and annoyed):* Do you have to squeeze me so tight?

LEOPOLDO *(with a pained smile):* You know ... among Chinese ...

GIRL: Look, I'm thirsty, I'm going to get something to drink.

LEOPOLDO *(leading the way):* Oh, allow me! Excuse us, please!

(Then, attempting to impress her) You know what I was just thinking? That some day you'll be here, right in this very theater, watching one of my plays.

GIRL: I like vaudeville.

LEOPOLDO *(with an indulgent smile):* How sweet! Did you ever see the upstairs of this place?

They have reached the refreshment tables, where cold cuts, cakes and pitchers of orangeade and lemonade have been set out. Among the waiters is Antonio. Someone tugs at Leopoldo's sleeve; it is the little maid from next door, costumed as a gypsy and wearing a mask.

MAID: You recognize me?

Leopoldo does not hide his surprise. He is embarrassed.

LEOPOLDO: Of course I recognize you!

He smiles, but does not know whether he ought to introduce the girls or not. He turns to the waiter.

LEOPOLDO: Two orangeades, please. *(To the maid)* Are you all by yourself?

MAID: No, I'm with some girls.

LEOPOLDO *(to the Chinese maiden):* Here you are. *(He hands her the orangeade, then turns back to the maid.)* I ... I decided to come just at the last minute ... *(Laughing nervously.)*

An embarrassed silence.

MAID: I know.

The Chinese maiden looks at the gypsy with ill-concealed disdain. She has finished her drink and sets the glass down on the table forcefully.

LEOPOLDO *(to the maid, to overcome his embarrassment):* That's a cute costume. *(To the Chinese maiden)* Shall we dance?

He puts the money on the table, clasps the Chinese girl around the waist and starts to dance. He throws a smile at the maid.

LEOPOLDO: Afterwards I'll dance with you!

The couple moves off on the dance floor. The little maid smiles back, somewhat humiliated.

MAID: Sure ... afterwards ...

Fausto and Sandra dance toward the tables.

FAUSTO: Like some cake, dear?

SANDRA *(in ecstasy):* No ... I'm dying of thirst! Some lemonade ...

The couple stops and Fausto asks Antonio:

FAUSTO: A lemonade, please ... *(Recognizing Antonio.)* Hello, Antonio.

ANTONIO *(pouring lemonade into a glass):* We're helping out here tonight.

FAUSTO *(distracted):* It's fun, isn't it?

MORALDO: Can I dance with my little sister?

Laughing excitedly, two ladies approach the refreshment tables, accompanied by a small gentleman in a tuxedo. One of the ladies, almost unrecognizable in her black evening gown, is Giulia, the wife of Fausto's employer. She is slightly tipsy.

GIULIA'S FRIEND: I could almost eat supper all over again. I'm starving ...

GENTLEMAN: Would you like some brandy, Giulia?

GIULIA *(laughing):* Oh no! I'm already feeling dizzy!

She suddenly notices Fausto's reflection in the mirror; he is watching her intensely, and in fact, her décolletage reveals an ample and exceedingly white bosom. She turns toward Fausto; moving into his roué character, he nods slightly at her.

Giulia is either actually high or else wishes to demonstrate that she can be informal with her employee. She suddenly takes a handful of confetti from her bag and flings it into Fausto's face with a shrill giggle.

Pleasantly surprised, Fausto spits out a few bits of confetti still stuck to his lips and, half-closing his eyes, chuckles.

FAUSTO: Having fun?

GIULIA: Lots.

Fausto drops his eyes very openly to Giulia's bosom. His nostrils flare.

FAUSTO *(indicating the dance floor):* Shall we?

Giulia immediately feels she has gone a little too far.

GIULIA *(serious):* No, thanks. I'm with some people ... *(Then, turning toward her husband, who is crossing the room:)* Michele!

She goes toward Michele, along with her two friends.

Fausto smiles enigmatically.

Two hours later, the affair is at its height. The band plays furiously, in a chaotic attempt to imitate American jazz style. The trumpet player rises for his solo.

Michele and Giulia dance together, laughing a little breathlessly.

Sandra's parents are dancing too, dignified and correct, doubling the band's tempo.

Fausto and Sandra dance as before, cheek to cheek.

In the center of the floor, Alberto is drinking from a bottle that a young man has handed him. He is already drunk and his antics are observed with great amusement by the couples who have formed a little circle around him.

Alberto shouts in imitation of the trumpet player.

The band's rhythm accelerates and its volume reaches a maximum.

Basement of the theater.

The ceiling vibrates under the feet of the dancers. Now and then a cloud of dust falls. The sound of the band upstairs is deafening.

A number of couples can be seen in the shadows.

One of the couples is Riccardo and his slave girl. Riccardo is tenderly kissing the girl's neck. She half closes her eyes and lets him do as he will.

RICCARDO *(softly):* Tomorrow I'm going to take you out for a ride in the country ...

Only one trumpet player is left; he is playing with boisterous abandon. The dance is at an end. The boxes are all empty. On the half-deserted dance floor, strewn with bags of confetti and streamers, the only dancers are Leopoldo, the little maid, the trumpet player and Alberto. His wig awry, Alberto drags himself clumsily and wearily along, leaning on a dummy figure.

Leopoldo hugs the little maid, who dances like a sack of potatoes.

Increasingly unsteady on his feet, Alberto dances with his arms tightly wrapped around the dummy. He kisses it and hugs it lovingly. Suddenly he stops. He seems about to throw up. He notices the impassive face of another dummy hanging from the ceiling and grimaces at it in disgust. By now at the end of his rope, Alberto makes his way slowly toward the exit of the theater, dragging the dummy along with him.

Lobby of the theater. Dawn.

Alberto stumbles out of the theater into the cold. The piazza in front of the theater is deserted. The trumpet can be heard sounding the last notes of the can-can.

Profound silence. Alberto leans up against a pillar in the lobby, waiting to regain his strength.

Alberto slips down along the pillar and comes to rest sitting at the base. He covers his face with one hand.

Moraldo pulls Alberto to his feet and begins to half lead, half carry him away. The girl follows, obviously annoyed by Moraldo's indifference to her.

MORALDO: Alberto, what's wrong? *(He comes closer.)* You feel sick?

(His head bowed, in annoyance.)

ALBERTO: No, I'm fine, I'm fine …

Moraldo comes still closer and starts to pull Alberto to his feet.

MORALDO: Come on, I'll take you home.

ALBERTO *(annoyed):* Get out of here! *(Seeing the Chinese maiden)* Go back to Peking!

MORALDO *(gently):* Come on, let's go, get up!

GIRL *(to Moraldo, softly):* Moraldo, leave him alone.

MORALDO: What d'you mean, leave him alone? It's Alberto, he's a friend of mine.

ALBERTO: Hell! *(Gets up.)*

Moraldo pulls Alberto to his feet and begins to half lead, half carry him away. The girl follows, obviously annoyed by Moraldo's indifference to her.

The dazed Alberto tries to appear normal.

ALBERTO: Shall we go swimming?

MORALDO *(as if addressing a lunatic):* Sure, we'll go swimming later ... Now let's go home ... We'll go together, eh?

The three walk off. Then Alberto stops and, wavering on his feet, stares hard at Moraldo.

ALBERTO: Who are you?

MORALDO: Moraldo.

ALBERTO: Who are you?

MORALDO: Moraldo.

ALBERTO: Uh-uh. You're nobody. You're all nobody. *(Collapses against Moraldo. Moraldo holds him up.)* All of you. All. Of course. What's got into your heads? *(Trying to free himself)* What's got ... lemme alone ... lemme alone ... lemme alone, you make me sick.

Moraldo finally releases him. Alberto starts to stagger off, still dragging along his dummy.

ALBERTO: I want to go by myself.

MORALDO: Alberto, you'll hurt yourself.

ALBERTO: I want to go by myself. I feel swell ...

MORALDO: Alberto, please.

ALBERTO: You're nobody. *(Turns and spits.)* You make me sick.

The girl again tries to get Moraldo away.

GIRL: Moraldo, please, let's go.

MORALDO: What d'you mean, let's go; I can't leave him here. *(To Alberto)* Can we go now? Can we go?

ALBERTO: Okay, let's go.

Followed by the girl, Moraldo goes up to Alberto and again helps him along.

ALBERTO: What d'you want from me?

MORALDO: Nothing. Nothing. Come on, let's go home.

ALBERTO: What d'you want from me?

MORALDO: Nothing, come on.

ALBERTO *(stopping)*: Oh, you know what, Moraldo? Listen. We got to get married.

MORALDO: Yes.

ALBERTO: We got to get married. Did you see Fausto? He's calm ... he's all set up, he's happy. In his own home ... we got to get married too.

Riccardo and his girl pass nearby and stop for a moment to greet them.

RICCARDO: Hi Alberto. Hi.

ALBERTO *(turning and shouting)*: You got to get married, Riccardo. You got to get married.

RICCARDO: So long, all right, all right, so long!

ALBERTO *(to Moraldo)*: Did you see? I told him, too. But you know what we'll do instead? We'll take a boat. We'll go to Brazil, eh? Think of it. Brazil! We'll take her too.

GIRL: Yes, you're right.

ALBERTO: Yes, I'm right: Brazil. We'll take a boat. *(Imitates a boat horn.)* I won't fall, I won't fall.

MORALDO: Yes, but let's go home now, all right?

ALBERTO: To Brazil ... on a gorgeous boat.

Moraldo starts off again with Alberto, who contines raving.

The girl protests.

GIRL: You're going to leave me here now?

MORALDO: But I can't leave him here. You come, too. Come on, you come, too.

They go off through the deserted piazza.

Street outside Alberto's house. Dawn.

The street is deserted. Paper streamers dangle from the electric lines. Not far up the street from Alberto's house a medium-sized Fiat is parked, its lights still on. The driver is the man we saw with Olga on the beach.

Alberto, Moraldo and the girl in Chinese costume turn the corner into the street and make their way to Alberto's door.

MORALDO *(paternally):* Here, Alberto. You're home now. You want me to come up with you?

ALBERTO *(leaning up against the wall):* I'm not going home, what should I do that for?

Behind him, a low voice vibrant with emotion:

OLGA: Alberto! ... Alberto!

Alberto turns and finds himself face to face with Olga. The girl is wearing her coat and carries a suitcase. Her eyes are red with weeping.

OLGA: I've been waiting for you all this time, Alberto ... I wanted to say goodbye ... Forgive me, Alberto ... Stay with Mama ... I'll always think of you ... Goodbye ... *(Olga kisses Alberto rapidly and goes toward the car. Softly, her voice trembling with tears)* Put some order in your life Alberto.

ALBERTO *(overcome, almost voiceless):* Olga, where are you going ... *(Turning to Moraldo)* Where's she going?

Before getting into the car, Olga turns and waves.

ALBERTO *(shouting):* Olga! Olga!! *(The car departs.)* Olgaaa!!

Alberto remains beside the door in a daze. He turns his gaze toward Moraldo, who has been deeply moved.

Alberto suddenly turns around and enters the house.

Inside Alberto's building. Dawn.

Alberto, panting, goes up the few steps to his own apartment, opens the door with some effort, and enters.

Dining room. Dawn.

His mother is seated at the table with her head in her hands. Her shoulders are shaken by sobs.

Alberto appears in the doorway. He stops, on the verge of tears.

ALBERTO *(sobbing hoarsely):* Mama ... what's happened?

MOTHER *(through her sobs):* You see ... she's gone ... How could she do this to me ... After all our sacrifices ... *(Starts sobbing again.)*

Alberto caresses his mother's shoulders, kisses her head ...

ALBERTO *(weeping):* Don't cry, Mama ... I'll never leave you, I'll always stay with you. *(The mother's sobs increase.)* And you'll see, she'll repent and come back ...

His mother shakes her head.

ALBERTO *(weeping, with anger):* And if she doesn't come back, all the better! What do you think? For that little bit of money she gave us! She should go, she should go! We don't need anybody ... I'll get a job myself!

At these words the mother stops crying and raises her head. She gazes at Alberto in some surprise.

MOTHER *(in a tiny little voice):* Really, Alberto?

ALBERTO: Of course!

MOTHER: Have you found something?

ALBERTO: Eh?

MOTHER: Have you found something?

Somewhat disturbed at having let slip such a precise promise, Alberto sniffles up his tears.

ALBERTO: No!

He collapses inert onto the armchair, sobbing ever more weakly.

Religious articles shop. Inside. Day.

Fausto enters the front door and looks around the shop, which is crowded with customers. (A group of nuns, another of friars, some seminary students and two little old ladies.)

(Carillon.)

As Michele, who is showing some statuettes to the nuns, sees Fausto enter, he darts a quick glance of reproof at the young man.

Fausto crosses the shop in no great hurry.

FAUSTO: Hello.

MICHELE *(curtly):* Ah!

Fausto is about to enter the back room when Michele's voice stops him.

MICHELE: Will you see what this lady wants?

FAUSTO *(turning):* What lady?

MICHELE: What d'you mean what lady? Over there!

He points to the little old lady who has timidly approached the center counter. Fausto stifles a yawn and leans casually over the counter.

FAUSTO: Yes?

OLD LADY: We wanted two little red tapers ... like the ones we bought two years ago ...

FAUSTO *(to Michele):* They want two little red tapers.

MICHELE *(containing his anger):* Well, get them! They're in there!

Fausto starts for the back room; as he passes Michele, he gives him a friendly, good-natured smile.

FAUSTO *(softly):* You enjoyed yourself last night, eh?

Michele holds back an annoyed gesture.

MICHELE *(softly but severely):* Listen, you better come in earlier in the morning.

FAUSTO *(confidentially):* Yes, I know. But ... Alberto's sister ran away ... *(He adds)* He's a friend of mine ...

MICHELE: Does she run away every morning? You've always got some excuse.

FAUSTO: And I have a little headache too.

MICHELE: Go on!

Slightly humiliated, Fausto enters the back room after waving at the old lady.

He goes toward the shelf on which several boxes of tapers are stacked. Selecting a box that lies beneath a number of others, he starts to pull it out with the sharp, elegant movement of the perfect clerk. The boxes above fall noisily to the floor.

(Sound of boxes falling.)

Michele flashes a glance at his wife and the two of them go to the back door to see what has happened.

Kneeling on the floor, Fausto is picking up the fallen tapers. He looks up at Michele and Giulia and smiles to beg forgiveness.

Michele, who has decided to control himself, gestures to his wife.

MICHELE: Help him.

Giulia bends down to gather up the tapers.

FAUSTO: Oh, no, Ma'am, I'm sorry.

Without answering, Giulia continues to pick up the tapers. Fausto finds her before him and cannot help staring at her hips and breasts.

Giulia feels his eyes on her and for a moment stops picking up the tapers. She feels annoyed and embarrassed, and rises as Fausto remains kneeling, gazing at her with a slight smile on his lips. Then Fausto gets up, too; the tapers have all been picked up by now.

Fausto opens his hand: a little pile of confetti rests on his palm.

Fausto "remembers": he smiles briefly, looks at Giulia, and, with a gesture which he intends to be of sophisticated complicity, tosses the confetti in Giulia's face.

She stares at him in astonishment and tacit resentment. She removes the confetti from her smock with short, sharp gestures. Nevertheless, she gives him a faint smile of courtesy.

GIULIA *(surprised):* Huh?

FAUSTO *(with a fatuous, mysterious smile):* What's given is returned...

Giulia stares severely at him for a moment, but is slightly embarrassed.

GIULIA *(curtly):* Carnival is over.

Fausto gazes warmly into her eyes, dropping his eyelids slightly.

FAUSTO *(significantly):* You, Ma'am, should always dress like you did last night.

Giulia leaves without answering.

Fausto smiles in self-satisfaction. Then he slowly reenters the shop carrying the box of tapers.

Now Fausto's eyes are fixed on Giulia, who is working at the desk in the back room.

The shop is empty.

Giulia raises her eyes from her work for a moment and sees Fausto staring at her. The young man's unusual behavior has put her on edge. To overcome her discomfort, Giulia turns to Fausto and speaks in the most natural way possible.

GIULIA: Please, Fausto, give me that set of receipts in the drawer.

Fausto smiles without taking his eyes from hers.

FAUSTO *(softly):* What drawer?

GIULIA: The drawer in the counter, there ...

Fausto nods approvingly and continues to interpret her intentions equivocally. He takes the receipts and enters the back room. He places the receipts on Giulia's desk and stands beside her as she continues to write without raising her head. Finally, rattled by Fausto's overbearing presence, she looks up at him.

FAUSTO *(softly):* Here are the receipts. You know I didn't sleep a wink last night? *(Pause)* I was dancing with you all night long ... in my dreams.

Giulia is obviously embarrassed. She takes some books from the desk and hands them to Fausto.

GIULIA *(firmly):* Put these in the bookshelf.

She has avoided looking at Fausto and the young man takes her reticence for sensual turmoil. Smiling, Fausto takes the books, starts for the bookshelf, then stops and smiles more broadly.

FAUSTO *(persuasively):* You help me.

For a moment Giulia pretends not to have heard his proposal, but she is obviously upset. She closes the ledger, gets up, and goes toward the shop.

But Fausto is waiting for her at the door and blocks her path.

Attempting to downgrade the incident as much as possible, she takes the books from Fausto and, without looking at him, says:

GIULIA *(in a choked voice):* Give them to me, I'll do it!

She starts to put the books on the shelf but Fausto, stepping quickly around her, puts his arms between the shelves and the woman, preventing her from passing.

FAUSTO *(seductively):* What a temperament! Only last night did I understand that you're a real woman.

Giulia's eyes dart rapidly hither and yon. Fausto is almost upon her, and she is forced to slip between his arm and the shelves.

GIULIA *(stammering):* But you're drunk!

She steps past him, bumping into him as she goes. Rapid and brusque though this contact is, it is enough to set Fausto in action. He approaches her.

FAUSTO *(murmuring):* Yes, drunk with you, with your flesh, with your perfume.

He kisses her on her neck by force.

GIULIA: Oh! That's enough of this silliness!

FAUSTO: Why do you want to make me think you don't like it?

GIULIA: No!

She emits a little choked cry. She escapes his embrace and slaps him. She rapidly tidies her hair and goes into the shop, flushed and breathless.

Michele enters the shop and goes up to his wife, rubbing his hands together.

MICHELE: The sun's out but it's awfully cold.

Fausto appears from the back room, adjusting his tie and trying to appear nonchalant. He avoids looking at Michele.

(Carrilon.)

After some silence, the door opens agains and a well-dressed woman of about forty enters, accompanied by a girl of about eighteen (her daughter). She nods and asks Michele:

CUSTOMER: Hello. Could I have some angels?

Closing time. The iron screen is rolled half-way down the door. Fausto has taken off his smock; he picks up his hat and coat and starts for the door.

FAUSTO: Goodbye, Sir. I'll go out this way.

Michele interrupts him.

MICHELE: No. Just a minute! Come up and have a drink with us. It's our wedding anniversary today. It's been fifteen years ...

He turns out the lights and opens a little door to the courtyard. He steps aside to let Fausto go first; Fausto is a little uncertain.

FAUSTO *(hesitating, and slightly diffident):* Best wishes ... I don't want to intrude ...

MICHELE: No, no. It's no intrusion at all. Come on.

FAUSTO: If I'd known I would have brought some flowers or something.

MICHELE: No, don't worry about that.

He points to the stairway, which leads from the store up to his apartment.

MICHELE: There ... go right on. We live upstairs. It's very convenient. Go on.

FAUSTO *(not knowing what else to say):* Thanks. Very kind of you.

The two men go up the stairs.

Michele's living room.

The room is dark. The hall light is suddenly turned on and illuminates the living room through the opaque panes of the door.

VOICE OF MICHELE: Come on in, come on in, just follow me.

The living room door opens and Michele turns on the light.

MICHELE *(calling):* Giulia! Would you bring the vermouth in here?

He takes three glasses and a tray from a cupboard.

Fausto remains in the doorway, looking at the room with interest. All his diffidence has evaporated.

FAUSTO: It's really nice here!

MICHELE *(turning):* You like it? It's not very elegant, but it's comfortable. Have a seat.

Fausto sits down in an armchair.

FAUSTO: I'm going to be setting up my own house now, too.

MICHELE *(darting him a rapid glance):* Oh, that's right ...

Giulia comes in with a bottle of vermouth and is somewhat surprised to see Fausto. She puts the bottle down without a word.

MICHELE: Oh, here's the vermouth.

GIULIA *(somewhat embarrassed):* I'm going back to the kitchen ... to finish up ...

MICHELE: Yes, dear. *(To Fausto)* She's a fine woman, isn't she?

Giulia walks out.

FAUSTO *(readily):* Oh yes, very. And ...

MICHELE: And? ...

FAUSTO *(not knowing what to say):* ... just fine!

Michele has been filling the glasses.

MICHELE: Ah yes! We're not young any more, but we get along fine together. We have only a few friends so we're almost always at home in the evenings ... in this room right here. Sometimes we even play cards! That should make you laugh, shouldn't it? Playing cards? Or else I read a book and my wife knits. And we don't bore each other. You know why? *(Pause)* Because we love each other. *(Pause)* But you can't understand that.

FAUSTO: Oh, I understand perfectly well.

MICHELE: No. You can't understand.

FAUSTO: Yes, I can.

MICHELE: No, you can't. And that makes me very sorry for you. And even sorrier for your poor little wife.

He takes some money from his pocket.

Fausto gulps for air as if wishing to speak.

FAUSTO *(aggressive and disdainful):* What do you mean? *(Pause.)*

Michele is moved to sudden wrath. He controls himself and throws the money on the table in front of Fausto.

MICHELE: Here, here's your pay for the month. Find some excuse for your family and your father-in-law. Say you didn't like it here ... that there was too much work ... say whatever you want ... You never have trouble finding excuses.

Fausto has risen, an uncertain smile on his face.

FAUSTO: Why are you firing me?

MICHELE: So you'll learn to live. I took you in like a brother and you've behaved like a rascal. And now go, because I have a great impulse to break your head!

FAUSTO *(feigning surprise and pain):* I never expected something like this from you.

He picks up the money.

MICHELE *(calling):* Giulia!

FAUSTO: No, look, forget it.

Fausto starts for the door; at the same time Giulia enters from the kitchen door and looks at her husband and Fausto rather tensely.

MICHELE: Mr. Moretti's leaving. He's not going to work for us any more. He's quitting his job.

FAUSTO *(with childish dejection):* Then I shouldn't come tomorrow?

MICHELE: No.

Silence.

FAUSTO *(softly):* Goodbye.

Michele and Giulia do not answer. After a moment's hesitation Fausto goes to the door.

FAUSTO *(to Giulia):* I was only joking, you know.

He goes out.

Café. Inside. Night.

Riccardo plays billiards with Caruso as Leopoldo keeps score. Fausto and Moraldo are leaning against the wall, talking together as they watch the game.

FAUSTO: I've lost my job.

MORALDO: What?

FAUSTO: On account of that stupid woman, the boss's wife.

MORALDO: What stupid woman?

FAUSTO: She fell for me! She was after me ... and since I wouldn't go along ... out of respect for the boss, too ... and then, she's old ... how could I possibly ... So then she put her husband against me. And today he found an excuse to fire me.

MORALDO *(shocked):* What excuse?

FAUSTO *(unprepared):* Eh?

MORALDO: He can't fire you just like that! That's too simple!

FAUSTO *(bitter and resigned):* No, he can, he can. Imagine, he told me "You find some excuse for your family" ... understand? *(Scornfully)* I'm supposed to find it ...

MORALDO *(with growing shock):* But this is absurd! You shouldn't have left! And then, he didn't give you severance pay. Anything? First of all he should have given you notice ... At least a month.

FAUSTO *(struck):* No, he didn't give me notice!

MORALDO: At least a month! He can't steal thirty thousand lire from you ... No, you can't fire people just like that today, you know. You work, you have a job, you know.

Moraldo continues to talk, but Fausto is no longer listening. He is distracted by another thought.

Cathedral Square. Night.

Moraldo and Fausto walk along side by side, their hands in their pockets and their heads lowered.

Fausto looks up at Moraldo, still uncertain whether or not to confide in him. Then he stops, as Moraldo goes a few steps further to drink at a fountain.

MORALDO: Ah, how good this water is. You're not drinking; aren't you thirsty?

FAUSTO: Listen, Moraldo. *(Moraldo stops and looks at Fausto, who gazes back intensely.)* Can you keep a secret?

Moraldo shrugs his shoulders, uncertain.

MORALDO: I don't know ... why?

FAUSTO *(coming close):* You said that my boss should have given me notice, right? *(Pause)* Well, I'm going to take my notice. *(Another pause)* Then we'll split it.

MORALDO: I don't understand.

FAUSTO *(mysteriously, instinctively looking about):* Would you be scared to go up on a roof, now?

MORALDO: What roof?

FAUSTO: A roof?

MORALDO *(increasingly uncertain and curious):* I don't know ... why?

FAUSTO *(impatient):* Look, are you scared?

MORALDO: No! ...

FAUSTO: Then let's go. Come with me!

Fausto starts off toward the end of the square.

Still hesitating, Moraldo remains there looking at him.

Fausto turns and repeats:

FAUSTO: Let's go.

Moraldo follows him.

Roof and courtyard of the religious articles store. Night.

Moraldo and Fausto crawl along the roof and let themselves down onto the skylight, which partially covers the courtyard of Michele's store.

Fausto goes first. They move cautiously, trying to make as little noise as possible. They have some difficulty sliding down the drainpipe into the courtyard, but manage it successfully.

Fausto helps Moraldo step down to the ground.

MORALDO *(panting, softly):* But ... but where are we?

FAUSTO *(softly):* Keep quiet! Don't talk. This is the courtyard. *(Pointing toward the house)* They're asleep; come on!

Fausto proceeds through the courtyard, trying to avoid stumbling over the packing cases, boxes, and packages that lie scattered all about.

Moraldo follows, increasingly irresolute. Fausto lights a match and gets his bearings. Moraldo makes his way over to him.

Fausto heads for a door locked with a great wooden bar.

FAUSTO *(whispering):* It's here.

With infinite caution he removes the bar. He hands the matches to Moraldo. Lights one.

Moraldo lights a match. Fausto opens the little door and comes upon a large pile of excelsior.

He enters the little room and brushes away some of the excelsior until he uncovers the face of a wooden statue of an angel. Fausto continues to remove the excelsior as Moraldo lights another match. The statue can now be seen in its entirety: it is about four feet long, of carved and painted wood. The angel is smiling.

Fausto turns happily to Moraldo.

MORALDO: What are you doing?

FAUSTO: Beautiful, isn't it?

MORALDO: But what is it?

FAUSTO: It's an angel! Now we have to get it out of here. You know how much this is worth? It's worth at least forty thousand lire. I saw the invoice. It's an antique.

The match burns out. In the dark, Moraldo's voice is terrified.

MORALDO *(appalled):* You're going to steal it?! *(Moraldo lights another match.)* Let's get out of here, Fausto.

FAUSTO *(softly, urgently):* I didn't steal it! When they unpacked the crates it got left here ... Nobody noticed. It's been here for two months! *(Pause)* And anyway, didn't you say I should have gotten notice? He's not giving it to me and we're taking it.

MORALDO *(hesitant):* But it's theft!

FAUSTO: Listen, Moraldo, I've got a family now. I need this money ... I've got a lot of things to do with it. If you're scared, say so. I'll manage by myself.

Moraldo does not answer.

After staring him in the eyes, Fausto bends down and picks the angel up in his arms.

FAUSTO: At least give me some light, will you?

Moraldo lights another match and the smiling face of the angel reappears next to Fausto's in the tremulous light.

FAUSTO: Look how beautiful it is!

MORALDO *(with a vague smile of tenderness and stupor, almost to himself):* Beautiful!

Street outside convent. Day.

A clear sunny morning. Giudizio, the station porter, is pushing along his wheelbarrow, on which stands the wooden angel, wrapped in a large sack.

Giudizio scampers merrily along sounding his trumpet.

About ten yards behind him come Fausto and Moraldo, who keep a close eye on Giudizio.

MORALDO *(alarmed):* Tell him to keep quiet!

FAUSTO *(calling softly):* Giudizio! Cut it out!

Giudizio turns, smiles daftly and mutters incomprehensibly as he points to the little doorway of a medieval convent.

Fausto and Moraldo approach the old building and Fausto pulls the bell rope. A bell tinkles somewhere inside.

(Sound of bell.)

Moraldo breathes slowly and the two friends avoid looking at each other.

The little door opens after a few moments and a young nun in spectacles puts her head out.

FAUSTO *(agressively cordial):* Good morning, Sister. Is the Mother Superior in?

NUN: Why?

FAUSTO *(with a traveling salesman's smile):* I'd like to show her something. *(Pointing to the sack on the wheelbarrow)* It's a real bargain ... May we talk to her?

At the word "bargain" the nun becomes a little suspicious. She darts a glance at the object and insists:

NUN: But what is it? Mother Superior's busy now.

MORALDO *(to Fausto, softly):* Fausto, let's go.

But Fausto does not yield. He turns to Moraldo:

FAUSTO: No, Moraldo. Show her ... show her. *(To the nun)* You'll see a beautiful thing!

Embarrassed, Moraldo hurriedly opens the sack and uncovers the angel's head.

Giudizio laughs happily.

The nun is startled.

FAUSTO *(smiling):* An angel. Made out of solid wood. It's been in our house but we have to sell it now ... it's a real bargain.

The appearance of the angel in the sack catches the nun unprepared. She comes out to examine the rosy face and blue eyes of the statue, then turns to look at the two friends once more with growing suspicion. Her eyes also reveal a mute, shocked reproof for this disrespectful way of carrying angels around.

Giudizio suddenly erupts with an undignified yell.

GIUDIZIO *(rapidly):* Angel, angel, angel, angel! ...

The nun starts in fear. She backs toward the door:

NUN: No we've already got lots of angels ... Goodbye.

FAUSTO: Just a minute!

But the door closes in his face. Fausto and Moraldo look silently at each other.

Giudizio has already closed the sack again; he starts off with the wheelbarrow and Fausto and Moraldo follow.

Hillside. Day.

Now the wheelbarrow is wending its laborious way up a little road that leads to a small hilltop near the city. Giudizio pulls it along like a horse, as Fausto and Moraldo, sweating profusely, push from behind. The statue totters and sways on the wheelbarrow.

The three pass in front of the garden of the large monastery which occupies the entire hilltop. Giudizio stops the wheelbarrow and points out a monk who is up in a tree pruning branches.

MONK: What do you want?

Fausto approaches the monk.

FAUSTO: Hello. How're things? Can I offer you a cigarette? Just a minute. Here, catch.

He takes out a cigarette and tosses it up to the monk, who catches it handily.

FAUSTO: Good catch! It's really nice up here! This is really living! ... Excuse me, what's your name?

MONK *(timidly):* Father Felice.

FAUSTO: Is the Father Guardian here?

MONK *(shaking his head.):* No.

FAUSTO: Oh; well ... when he's not here, who looks after things? ...

MONK: Me.

FAUSTO: Oh, that's fine ... *(Pauses, solemnly.)* I'd like to offer you a very good deal. Would you be interested in a really magnificent statue, painted, suitable for an altar?

The monk climbs out of the tree and comes up to the three.

MONK *(curtly):* Is that it?

FAUSTO: Yes. *(To Moraldo)* Show it to him.

Moraldo uneasily and hurriedly opens the sack, uncovering the angel's face.

FAUSTO: Look what a beautiful thing. Look what an expression.

The monk looks at the statue. After a moment of silence, he stares at Fausto.

MONK: Where did you get it?

Moraldo's guilty face is quite eloquent. But Fausto's courage does not desert him.

FAUSTO: We had it at home ... But there isn't any proper place for it, you know ... so we decided to sell it.

The monk glances again at the statue and then back at Fausto.

MONK *(slowly, harshly):* No. We don't need it up here.

He turns his back on the three and goes back to his tree, gathering up a bundle of dry sticks.

Seaside. Evening.

SPEAKER: That day they couldn't sell the statue. In the evening, Fausto and Moraldo entrusted it to Giudizio with infinite warnings.

A street with poor houses and shacks in the seaside district. Night is falling. Giudizio, Fausto, and Moraldo walk along in the distance. They stop. Giudizio, at the handles of the wheelbarrow, listens to Fausto and Moraldo, and gestures warmly to reassure them.

Beach. Day.

Giudizio, seated on a pile of sand with a bit of bread in his hand, ecstatically observes the statue standing on his doorsill.

Beside him, two dogs wander about sniffing the ground.

After gazing at length at the statue, Giudizio rises, takes the statue and carries it out on the beach, where he sets it down on a pile of sand.

Then he admires the effect, gazing at it with love and admiration; he caresses it in fascination.

GIUDIZIO *(to himself):* Angel! ...

Entrance and hallway of Sandra's house. Night.

Sandra's father enters like a fury, slamming the door behind him.

Dining room. Night.

(Sound of door slamming.)

Sandra, her mother, Fausto and Moraldo are sitting at the table; the seat at the head of the table is empty.

SANDRA: Here's Papa.

At the sound of the terrific crash of the door, they remain immobile, their soup spoons poised and their eyes fixed on the door, which after a moment is flung open by Sandra's father.

Mr. Rubini stops for a moment on the doorsill, breathing hard. He slams the door shut. Then, dissimulating his true intention, he walks around the room looking at nothing until he suddenly leaps toward Moraldo.

The maneuver fails because Moraldo, who has understood immediately, jumps up in time and begins to circle around the table.

Having lost his initial advantage, Mr. Rubini now has the entire length of the table separating him from his son.

SANDRA'S FATHER *(trying to keep his voice normal, with effort):*

Moraldo, come here ... Let me get you or it'll be even worse for you!

Fausto, the first to recover from the surprise, is serving himself a chop, though his eyes remain glued on his father-in-law.

Moraldo is still circling around the table.

MORALDO *(with the frightened air of feigned innocence):* But why, what have I done?

SANDRA'S FATHER: You devil! What have you done? *(Pointing to Moraldo and Fausto)* Thieves! Out of my house! Both of you!

SANDRA'S MOTHER *(horrified):* But what's happened?

SANDRA'S FATHER *(choking with wrath):* They stole a whole statue! ... My son ... And that other beggar there ... Like two thieves! The police were coming! *(Pointing to Fausto)* ... And that filthy pig ... has been bothering the wife of my friend ... The shame of it ...

Fausto ceases cutting his chop. Sandra stands up, trembling, bursts out in tears and runs out.

Fausto, still seated, answers with his voice raised.

FAUSTO: They've told you a bunch of lies. I'm surprised a man like you could listen to them. I'm very surprised.

SANDRA'S FATHER: And you dare raise your voice too!

FAUSTO *(rising and slamming the silverware down on his plate):* Yes I'm raising it! You treat me like a kid of five. I'm thirty years old. *(He flings the plate off the table angrily and takes his jacket from the back of the chair.)* You can keep your chops, you won't see any more of me! Not any more.

He leaves the room in a rage.

Sandra's room. Night.

Sandra is lying on the bed in the dimly lit room. She clutches a crumpled handkerchief in her hand; her eyes are red with weeping.

The door opens softly behind her and Moraldo appears. He watches his sister sobbing and then sits down on the bed beside her.

MORALDO *(softly):* Sandra ...

The girl does not answer; her shoulders are still shaken by sobs.

MORALDO *(bending over her):* ... Sandra ... It wasn't his fault. It was her ... his boss's wife who was after him. And after, she put her husband against him ... *(Pause)* Sandra, do you hear me?

Sandra continues to sob.

Sandra raises her tear-filled eyes.

SANDRA *(with hope in her voice):* Really?

MORALDO: Yes, it was her ... because Fausto wouldn't go along with her.

SANDRA: Oh?

She looks at Moraldo again.

MORALDO: Because Fausto wouldn't even look at her. And they wouldn't even give him any money. So we thought we'd take that statue ...

SANDRA *(smiling weakly through her tears):* Really he wouldn't go along with her?

MORALDO: Yes. I swear to you.

Sandra gazes at Moraldo and begins to dry her tears.

SANDRA *(with an anguished smile):* And where has he gone now?

MORALDO: He's out in the garden.

Garden of Rubini house. Night.

Fausto, seated on a broken crate at the edge of the garden, is smoking a cigarette in silent wrath. The sound of footsteps on the gravel arouses him, and he turns to see Sandra standing before him.

SANDRA: Fausto!

She smiles tenderly at him, then comes closer.

FAUSTO: I'm waiting for Moraldo and then I'm going. Tell your father he won't see me any more ... I don't want to be a burden to anybody.

SANDRA: Fausto, what are you saying? Moraldo's told me everything...

FAUSTO *(somewhat alarmed)*: What everything?

SANDRA: Yes, I'm going to tell Papa ... that it was that woman's fault ...

FAUSTO: Don't let's talk about it ...

SANDRA: No, they have to know!

Fausto lowers his eyes, touched by Sandra's innocence in spite of himself. Sitting down beside him, she takes a package from her pocket.

SANDRA: Here ... it's your chop ... you haven't eaten a thing ...

To strike a face-saving attitude, Fausto gazes at the sky.

FAUSTO *(moved)*: Hell!

And he takes the sandwich.

SANDRA *(after a pause)*: Why did you take that statue? Did you need money? ... You could have told me! Why didn't you confide in me?

Fausto, who has begun to eat his sandwich, is gradually overcome by self-pity. He sighs heavily at Sandra.

SANDRA *(with tears in her voice, tenderly)*: We have to tell each other

everything ... we have to be close ... we're all by ourselves ...
Mama's so kind ... but she treats me as if I were still four
years old ... And papa's always so busy ... he doesn't know
me at all ... I have only you, Fausto! *(Her voice dies away in
a whisper of desperation and she weeps.)* If you leave too ...

Strangled by emotion, Fausto embraces her.

FAUSTO: Sandra ... don't talk like that ...

He awkwardly kisses her hair.

Sandra happily leans up against him, still sobbing.

SANDRA *(whispering):* You still love me? You love our child?

FAUSTO *(his eyes filled with tears):* My little Sandra ... Sandra, it's
our child.

SANDRA *(trembling):* Then ... you'll stay with me?

FAUSTO *(chewing his sandwich, moved):* Yes. Yes.

SANDRA: Then come.

FAUSTO: No, no.

SANDRA: Let's go in.

FAUSTO: No, let me alone.

SANDRA: We'll go to Papa, come.

They go back to the house arm in arm.

SPEAKER: So Fausto was forgiven and he settled down to looking
leisurely for a new job.

Café. Day.

*Fausto, at the billiard table, aims a good shot and knocks down all
the pins as Leopoldo, Riccardo, Alberto, and Moraldo look on.*

Dining room, Rubini home. Day.

Sandra's parents and aunts, Moraldo, Sandra and Fausto gather around the maid, who is holding a new-born infant.

SPEAKER: Anyway, the family took a little less notice of Fausto now that the baby was born ... a beautiful boy ... he looked like his mother, like his father and also a little like his grandparents, his great-aunts and like Moraldo. *(The adults are all making faces and smiling at the child.)* Sandra was happy. And one day, she slipped out ...

Fausto's father's house. Day.

Sandra is sitting at the kitchen table with the child in her arms.

SPEAKER: And went to visit her father-in-law to show him Moraldino.

Fausto's father sits across the table from her. Both of them gaze spellbound at the baby. The father feels awkward and embarrassed, and for the first time we see him smile.

LITTLE SISTER: I've put the coffee on.

FATHER: Good girl, good girl.

LITTLE SISTER *(to Moraldino):* Moraldino, Moraldino, why are you so fat?

SANDRA: Yesterday he said "blue." I wonder what he meant?

Fausto's little sister brings over the coffee cups on a tray.

FAUSTO'S FATHER: And what about Fausto? Has he found a job?

SANDRA *(somewhat embarrassed):* Well, yes ... it seems so. Anyway it's a matter of days. *(To change the subject, Sandra gets up.)* Excuse me, Papa, I'll go see about the coffee.

FAUSTO'S FATHER *(getting up too):* No, no. I'll go!

SANDRA: No, let me, Papa!

LITTLE SISTER: Sandra, can I hold him a little?

SANDRA: All right, if you want to. But be careful. Don't let him fall.

She hands the baby to Fausto's sister, who stands stock-still out of joy and responsibility, and kisses her nephew.

LITTLE SISTER: Moraldino, my handsome Moraldino, give your auntie a little kiss.

Fausto's father, who has been watching apprehensively, takes the child from his daughter's arms.

FAUSTO'S FATHER *(murmuring):* Give him to Grandpa for a minute.

LITTLE SISTER: Oh no, Papa. You don't know how to hold him. *(Giggling)* You don't hold babies that way.

Street outside Moraldo's house. Night.

Moraldo is sitting on a bench along the silent, deserted avenue. The young railroad boy is with him. They are watching the stars and Moraldo answers a question the boy has asked him.

MORALDO: I don't know that one.

BOY *(pointing to another star):* That's the one that's furthest away of all, isn't it?

MORALDO: And it's called Sirius. Yes.

BOY *(continuing to gaze spellbound at the stars):* And there must be people there, like here ...

MORALDO *(shaking his head):* Well, I don't think so.

BOY *(turning to Moraldo):* Would you go live there?

MORALDO: Oh, I would, sure.

BOY *(smiling):* Oh come on!

MORALDO: I would too!

BOY *(getting up):* Coming along with me?

MORALDO *(getting up in turn):* Sure I'm coming along.

They go off together toward the station.

SPEAKER: The nights were warmer now ...

Piazza with fountain. Night.

Moraldo walks alone through the piazza, heading toward the fountain. A bell is tolling in the distance.

SPEAKER: ... and spring was already in the air.

Bertucci Theater. Inside.

On the stage, eight chorus girls are performing a dance number, accompanied by the band that had played at the Carnival dance. The number is coming to an end.

The theater is filled to overflowing. Sitting near the front are Alberto, Riccardo, Fausto, Moraldo, and Leopoldo.

The dance ends and the black silk curtain is drawn. The audience applauds wildly.

All the Vitelloni are applauding, too, except for Fausto, who has assumed the blasé air of an experienced theater-goer.

The stage lights dim as a voice announces solemnly over the microphone.

LOUDSPEAKER: And now, we present a great name and a great spirit, Commendatore Sergio Natali.

(Drum-roll.)

LEOPOLDO *(extremely excited, whispering softly to his friends):* Here he is now ... Now behave yourselves, please ...

Spotlighted against the black curtain appears a tall, heavy, elderly man correctly dressed in black, with his gray hair disheveled in the manner of an artist.

Leopoldo, deeply moved, applauds warmly and the rest of the audience follows suit.

(Enthusiastic applause.)

In the silence that follows, the ostensibly touched Natali thanks the audience by bowing to the right, to the left, and to the center, and then looks up to the balcony.

THE OLD ACTOR: Thank you ... thank you ... thank you ... *(Then, closing his eyes and extending his arm, he announces)* I shall recite "Youthful Fancy."

Leopoldo, already moved, turns to his friends.

LEOPOLDO *(murmuring):* He's great ... He's great!

But Alberto cannot help commenting.

ALBERTO: This is Natali?

LEOPOLDO: Yes.

ALBERTO *(softly):* But look, he's really ugly, you know?

Leopoldo urges him to silence with an annoyed and slightly hysterical gesture.

A child of about seven is pushed out from the wings and, remaining at some distance from the actor, he speaks in a piping voice.

CHILD: Papa?

The old actor approaches the child and caresses his head, feigning intense emotion.

OLD ACTOR *(declaiming):* Little boy, your father has already returned. He is here among us, mingling with the people. He watches you, he smiles at you, and he has touched you. And you, little boy, have not been aware of him.

CHILD: But why, Grandfather?

OLD ACTOR: Because you are innocent. Because Papa left at springtide. Like your Grandfather left, as a lieutenant, with flowers, with song and with a flag. *(Singing softly)* "Sound, bugle, sound, my bugle ..."

The old actor continues his song, gradually increasing the volume, as a drum-roll rises from the orchestra in imitation of the march of soldiers.

(Drum-roll.)

A wave of emotion surges through the audience.

Leopoldo bends forward with his eyes starting out of his head and follows the scene with the greatest attention.

SPEAKER: This is the evening that Leopoldo has been waiting so long for. The great actor has read his play and will be waiting for him in his dressing room after the performance.

(The music and the drum-roll increase in volume.)

The chorus girls are back on stage now, busbies on their heads and swords hanging at their bare thighs, marching up and down as the old actor, drawn up stiffly at attention, continues to sing.

OLD ACTOR *(singing):* ... Youth fades away, love fades awaaay!!!

The orchestra trumpeter suddenly sounds a fanfare and the chanteuse appears from behind the backdrop, where the dancers have lined up. She is scantily clad as "Italy," with a turreted crown over her long flowing locks and a filmy veil draped over her shoulders.

Her appearance inspires wild applause from the audience.

The Vitelloni lean forward to watch. Alberto and Riccardo exchange appreciative glances.

(The orchestra plays "Fly, dove".)

The chanteuse opens her arms to embrace the whole audience.

CHANTEUSE *(singing):* Fly, white dove, fly ...

CHORUS GIRLS *(singing):* Tell her I'll be home ...

CHANTEUSE *(as above):* Tell her not to cry ...

CHORUS GIRLS *(as above):* ... I'll never more roam.

Now all the performers are downstage.

(Drums.)

The drums beat four notes and the orchestra plunges into the finale.

CHORUS: Wings of the dove/ Carry my love!/ Through the night/ Carry my love/ Wings of the dove/ To my heart's delight!!

Backstage. Night.

SPEAKER: The great moment had come ...

The entranced Leopoldo moves through the backdrops and the bustling activity of the stagehands, followed by his four friends. All keyed up, he continues down a corridor, the friends still following along.

Natali, the old actor, suddenly appears in front of a doorway that is covered by a tattered curtain. His make-up has been partially removed; he is wrapped in a shabby, patched robe and carries a candle.

OLD ACTOR *(in a resonant and cordial voice):* Ah, it's you! With some friends. Do come in, do come in. Please sit down. Please, please come in. *(Loudly)* Bring some chairs.

The young men, somewhat awkward and embarrassed, enter the little room

RICCARDO AND ALBERTO: Don't take the trouble ... we can stand ...

OLD ACTOR: Excuse the candle, but in these awful little provincial theaters they steal all the light bulbs.

LEOPOLDO: Oh, I know, sir, but don't worry about it.

OLD ACTOR *(holding out a pack of cigarettes):* Have a cigarette? Italian cigarettes ... because ... for the voice, the Americans are terribly dangerous ...

As the four friends accept the cigarettes and light up, Leopoldo is filled with emotion and joy.

LEOPOLDO: Sir, I'm a great admirer of yours ...

RICCARDO: I saw you in a picture: "The Two Foscari's."

OLD ACTOR: Oh, yes! But you know, they cut everything out in the editing. Do please sit down a moment. I'll finish taking off my make-up, if you don't mind.

Leopoldo sits down and begins again.

LEOPOLDO: The first time I saw you ... in Bologna ... in 1943 ... it was an unforgettable evening ... You revealed Ibsen to me!

OLD ACTOR *(thoughtfully and bitterly):* Oh Ibsen, those were the days. It seems only yesterday! My dear friend ... it's no easy thing to direct a company ... and you see me now in what I'd call a vacation period ... a temporary thing ... Because for next year I'm now organizing a really exceptional troupe ... just think, I'll probably have Ferrari and maybe Gassman.

A woman is heard laughing, and (as the old actor continues talking offscreen) a dancer appears in the doorway of another dressing room and appraises the handsome Fausto with an expert's eye.

Leopoldo emits a sound of approval.

LEOPOLDO *(to Alberto):* Did you hear that? Ferrari and Gassman, he's going to have!

OLD ACTOR: And I want to present new works ... of young people ... because of the subsidies, but also because I like a battle ... And speaking of new works, I've read your play. Well really, just part of it, because you can well imagine that I'm always so busy. The theater is a tyrant ...

The old man stares lengthily at Leopoldo, who is eagerly awaiting his opinion.

Then the old actor nods with grave geniality.

OLD ACTOR: There's ... there's ...

LEOPOLDO *(rising slowly and swallowing hard):* Really ... you liked it?

OLD ACTOR *(touching his forehead):* There's this ... and *(Touching his heart)* and this too ...

LEOPOLDO: Sir ...

Leopoldo's happy smile borders on anguish. He cannot find words. He swallows and gazes ecstatically at his friends .

Restaurant. Inside. Night.

One table in the otherwise deserted restaurant is occupied by Leopoldo, Riccardo, Alberto, Fausto, and Moraldo, with the old actor eating his supper at the head of the table. Natali's eyes are still made up. Leopoldo is spiritedly reading his script; his voice and gestures are animated by an unusual forcefulness. He is truly immersed in the poetic wave which he believes he has evoked with his creation.

Leopoldo's friends sit around the table but are not eating. Alberto has some cake before him and the others have liqueur glasses or coffee cups.

The old actor listens approvingly to Leopoldo's recitation as he eats with great appetite. He gestures repeatedly to the young men to pass him the bread, the wine, and the salt.

LEOPOLDO *(reading from the script):* "Roberto: I'm a child of my age. There are no more authorities on my pedestals. I don't know if you understand, Frida. *Frida:* I think I understand, Roberto, that your pride is devouring you. *Roberto (laughing):* Ha, ha, ha ... What is left for pride to devour in a soul already consumed? *Frida:* Oh, you are blind! Only fear can save you!"

OLD ACTOR *(repeating):* "Oh, you are blind! Only fear can save you!"

LEOPOLDO *(to the old actor):* Magnificent! But this is a line of Frida's ... *(Continuing)* "Frida: In the silence of your desert, do you not hear a voice calling you? *Roberto (ironically):* Your voice, Frida? *Frida:* No, God's."

Leopoldo delivers this last line and lets the page fall to the table.

LEOPOLDO: That's the end of the second act.

RICCARDO: It's terrific, isn't it?

MORALDO: Fine, isn't it? Isn't it fine?

Leopoldo picks up the rest of the script.

LEOPOLDO: Shall I begin the third act?

OLD ACTOR: Do!

LEOPOLDO: Act Three. Scene One ...

(The chanteuse laughs.)

They all turn toward the door, where the chanteuse has entered along with two of the chorus girls. She laughs in falsetto.

A gust of wind whips up the corners of the tablecloths.

At the actor's table, Natali is obviously annoyed by the appearance of the chanteuse.

OLD ACTOR: The door, please ...

One of the chorus girls closes the door as the chanteuse, still laughing, glances at the group of friends and sits down at the table beside theirs. Leopoldo quivers with anger at this interruption, which may postpone the reading of his play.

LEOPOLDO: May I go on? Act Three.

CHANTEUSE: Ha, ha, ha ... Waiter!

The waiter hurries over to the women's table.

CHANTEUSE *(to Natali):* Hello, Natali.

OLD ACTOR *(to Chanteuse):* Hello ... *(To Leopoldo)* Go right on!

LEOPOLDO *(encouraged, starts reading again):* "The scene is the same as the first act. Roberto is sitting in front of the fireplace watching the gaily blazing flames. Frida is at the window, staring at the sunset, which gilds the dunes. They hear the screaming of the seagulls. As if suddenly chilled, Frida turns. She is tired and worn."

Fausto, Alberto, Ricardo, and Moraldo are watching the chanteuse and the two chorus girls.

Fausto smiles at the chanteuse ... who returns a languid gaze and a little laugh.

(As Leopoldo reads, the chanteuse repeatedly laughs and gives her order ad lib to the waiter.)

Moraldo notices and, despite himself, turns serious for a moment.

Leopoldo looks up from the script at the actor, who is staring straight ahead seriously and eating a custard dessert.

LEOPOLDO *(resuming):* "She approaches Roberto. *Frida:* There'll be no moon tonight."

Half an hour later.

Alberto, Fausto, Riccardo and Moraldo have moved over to the women's table.

Alberto is on his feet with his glass in his hand, giving an imitation of a famous actor.

ALBERTO: I love wine. And devil take the man who won't drink with me!

Uproarious laughter.

The chanteuse feeds Fausto a peeled banana, with allusive and obscene intent.

Another girl asks Alberto:

CHORUS GIRL: Can you do Gary Cooper?

RICCARDO *(shouting to Alberto):* Alberto, do the saw, do the saw, Alberto.

ALBERTO: I can do a saw real good. But close your eyes, everybody.

RICCARDO: Everybody quiet, this is good.

Placing one hand across his other arm, Alberto imitates the movement of a handsaw, which he accompanies with appropriate noises.

This performance, too, is greeted by uproarious laughter. The girls are highly amused. One of them gets up and puts a napkin on her head.

GIRL *(simpering):* Now I'll do an imitation. My grandmother!

Alberto immediately leaps upon her and wraps her in his arms.

ALBERTO: My sweet little grandma, I'll never leave your side.

A third girl, evidently struck by Moraldo's charm, caresses his head.

GIRL *(with a toothpick in her mouth):* Can't you do any imitations? What's the matter with you, always so serious? *(Then,*

turning to her friend:) You know, I really like this little
fellow. *(Inspired)* He's a very refined type of guy!

CHANTEUSE: You're right, he is.

*The group's attention is caught by the voice of Leopoldo, who
declaims a key passage of his play to the old actor.*

LEOPOLDO *(reading passionately):* "Not even crime! Nothing can
horrify me any more! And yet, I remember ..."

*Leopoldo's friends and the girls burst out in amused, insolent
laughter.*

*Fausto whispers something in the chanteuse's ear. Moraldo watches
him disapprovingly.*

RICCARDO *(rising):* Hey, kids, there's a radio here. I'll turn it on.

The chanteuse laughs at what Fausto has said and answers jokingly.

CHANTEUSE *(imitating a Neapolitan accent):* Ué, ué-ué-ué, you
shouldn't say such things, ha-ha-ha ...

*The radio is playing a dance tune; Fausto pulls the chanteuse to her
feet and invites her to dance. Squeezing her tightly against him, he
winks at Moraldo. Moraldo, serious, somewhat sad and embarrassed, lowers his eyes.*

*At the actor's table, Natali is obviously annoyed by the merrymaking
of the young men and the girls. He suddenly gets up, picks up his
coat and heads for the door.*

Leopoldo hurries to follow him. Alberto sees him at the door.

ALBERTO *(calling):* Leopoldo! Where are you going?

LEOPOLDO *(excited):* Later, later. I'll tell you later. He's had a poetic
inspiration ... a magnificent idea, an artist's inspiration.

He goes out.

Street outside restaurant. Night.

*The night is very dark and windy. The cones of light from the street
lamps tremble on the asphalt.*

The old actor lifts his nose and breaths deeply.

OLD ACTOR: Wind from the sea ... Wind of the night! *(He starts off,
with Leopoldo at his side.)* Your friends disappoint me. Who
loves not art, loves not life ... *(Pause)* Is this the way to the
sea?

LEOPOLDO: Yes, sir.

OLD ACTOR *(stopping):* Let's not be so formal ... among artists ...
(Starting off again) Your Frida is a monumental character,
perfect ... Just the thing for Ferrari ... Just the thing. In fact
I'm going to write her tonight about it and she'll certainly
accept. If the third act is like the first two you read ... It's just
the thing we need, my boy ... What's your name?

LEOPOLDO: Leopoldo, sir.

OLD ACTOR *(solemnly):* Leopoldo! In two months' time, you will come to Milan!

LEOPOLDO *(stops, strangled by a sudden wave of emotion):* Really, sir? You really mean that?

OLD ACTOR: Call me Sergio.

LEOPOLDO *(his voice choking and trembling):* You really mean that, sir?

OLD ACTOR *(into the wind):* Come, Leopoldo, let's go read the third act ...

The two men walk along leaning into the wind, their heads lowered; the actor holds his hat on with his hand.

LEOPOLDO: Sir, you don't know ... you don't know, Sergio ... what your words mean for me ... I was about to give up, to abandon all ... My boyish dreams, my hopes.

OLD ACTOR: The sea, the sea. Which way.

LEOPOLDO: It's hard, you know, to live in the midst of people who cannot understand, in this deadly provincial life, deaf to all art, to every voice ... One's all alone ... even one's friends don't really understand; their interests are more material ... more contingent ... women ... money ... Winter never passes. Look, everything's all over by midnight. How can an artist dream his dreams here, how can he live ... And so the years roll by, and one morning you wake up ... you were a boy and you're a boy no longer ...

The old actor, who has been listening to Leopoldo's speech without ever turning to him, begins whistling.

The old actor whistles "Fly, dove".

A sharp gust of wind carries off Leopoldo's hat. He races breathlessly after it, continuing to speak, and finally catches it.

LEOPOLDO: Ah, but now ... now it's all over! I knew I shouldn't give up! In two months I'll be in Milan ... or wherever you want.

The old actor is still walking on. Leopoldo calls him and catches up to him, taking his arm as they go toward the sea.

LEOPOLDO: Sergio! Sergio!

Seaside with pier. Night.

Leopoldo and the actor stand side by side on the seashore drive. After a few moments, the actor looks around.

OLD ACTOR: Ah, the sea! Is that the pier over there?

LEOPOLDO *(pulling up his collar):* Yes!

OLD ACTOR *(impatiently):* You have to read me the fourth act! Let's go ...

Followed by Leopoldo, he goes toward the pier.

Leopoldo seems somewhat puzzled. He clutches his script to his breast.

LEOPOLDO: Sir, ah, Sergio, but ... where are you going?

OLD ACTOR: We'll find a place down there.

LEOPOLDO: But it's dark down there ... Sir ...

But the old man has already started down.

(Sound of wind and waves.)

Leopoldo stops, somewhat confused and worried.

Then the actor turns to look at Leopoldo; a revealing and bloodcurdling smile has appeared on his ravaged face.

For a moment the two men stare at each other in silence.

OLD ACTOR: Come! come!

OLD ACTOR *(still smiling that same atrocious smile):* Are you possibly afraid of me?

Leopoldo seems bolted to the spot. Then he begins to back away.

He takes another step backwards.

OLD ACTOR *(calling):* Poldy! Poldy! Where are you going? I was just joking. Come here. Poldy! Ha-ha-ha-ha ...

Leopoldo does not answer. Through the dark he can see the tragic, grotesque face of the old actor, immobile in the whipping wind.

Bitterness and infinite disgust choke his throat and freeze his heart. He turns suddenly and runs back toward the town.

Hotel room. Night.

The drowsy head of the chanteuse emerges from the sheets. With her eyes half closed, she offers her lips to Fausto, who bends down to kiss her goodbye.

FAUSTO: So long!

CHANTEUSE *(sleepily):* So long, baby. Put your coat on. Don't catch a cold ...

FAUSTO *(softly):* Tomorrow I'll come to the station to say goodbye. So long.

She falls back on the bed, fast asleep. Fausto crosses the dimly lit room and goes out into the hall.

Piazza outside the hotel. Night.

(Bell tolls.)

The bell rings three times over the deserted and wind-swept piazza. Moraldo is standing near the fountain, his collar raised against the cold. He turns to look at the hotel entrance.

Fausto comes out of the hotel. He starts across the piazza, but

Moraldo comes toward him. As Fausto sees him he stops in surprise

FAUSTO: What are you doing here?

MORALDO: Waiting for you.

FAUSTO: Oh, thanks a lot, that was nice of you.

MORALDO: I think it's better if we go back home together.

FAUSTO: Of course!

They walk along side by side in silence.

Moraldo's unusual attitude makes Fausto a little uneasy. To overcome this, he says:

FAUSTO: What a woman! You know what she told me? That if I can sing she'll hire me. It's not a bad life, you know. You travel, you have fun, you're free, no worries ... women all over the place ... *(He begins to dance and sing.)* "Ah, those were the day ..."

Moraldo gazes at him in reproof. Fausto suddenly stops.

FAUSTO: What about you?

MORALDO *(not looking at him):* Me? ... Nothing. Nothing.

FAUSTO: Why not? She wasn't bad looking at all, you know. *(Slightly irritated)* What's the matter with you anyway?

MORALDO: Nothing. I was thinking ...

FAUSTO: About what?

MORALDO: About Sandra.

He starts walking again, head lowered. Fausto follows him.

FAUSTO: Oh ... oh, then that's why you waited for me? Eh? Come on, answer ...

Moraldo does not answer. He continues to walk along with his head lowered.

Stairway in Rubini house. Night.

Moraldo and Fausto tiptoe up the stairs. His face grim, Fausto stops to say goodnight to Moraldo.

FAUSTO *(softly):* Good night.

MORALDO *(softly):* Wipe off your face, you're full of lipstick … *(Fausto rapidly takes out his handkerchief and wipes his cheek)* The other one.

Fausto wipes his other cheek. Without waiting to be thanked, Moraldo starts for his room. Fausto watches him go, then opens the door of his own room and enters on tiptoe.

Sandra's and Fausto's room. Night.

The room is dark. Sandra is in bed; her eyes stare straight ahead. The baby is in bed with her.

Fausto, who has not noticed that his wife is awake, stops in front of the mirror and rubs his handkerchief over his cheek, dampening it with spit. Then as he starts to take off his jacket, he notices that her eyes are wide open and that she is staring at him.

Fausto is surprised and dismayed.

FAUSTO: Oh, Sandra … *(Pause; then a sickly smile)* You're not asleep?

Then, to break the embarrassing tension, he leans smilingly over the child.

FAUSTO *(whispering jokingly):* What a face, what a cute little fella …

He reaches out to caress the child's head, but Sandra's angry, choked-up voice stops him.

SANDRA: Don't touch him!

FAUSTO *(surprised):* Why not?

*He pulls back his hand in embarrassment as Sandra, overcome by
her anguish, turns away and sobs quietly. For a moment Fausto
hopes that she will stop, but he must finally assume some attitude.*

FAUSTO *(with an astonished tone):* What are you doing now? You're
crying?

SANDRA *(biting her lips to keep back her tears, she begs desperately):*
Go away. Get out of here! Go away! ... Get out of here! ...

*Fausto sits down on the bed and bends toward his wife, trying to
caress her shoulder; and speaking in a tone of voice which he tries to
make heartstruck and surprised.*

FAUSTO: Sandra! Listen, Sandra. You're going to wake the baby.
(Sandra continues to sob without answering) Sandra. *(No
answer. Heartstruck, but decisive):* Well tell me, what have I
done now?

*A louder sob answers this last question; a long, desperate sob which
shakes Sandra's whole body and silences Fausto.*

Moraldo's room. Night.

*Moraldo, still half dressed, is sitting on his bed. Then he gets up and
comes over to the wall dividing the two rooms; pale and tense, he
listens to Sandra weeping.*

Sandra's and Fausto's room. Night.

*Two hours later. A cock crows in the distance. The room is
somewhat brightened now by the weak light entering through the
closed shutters.*

*Her face ravished by tears, Sandra raises her head from the pillow to
look at the sleeping Fausto. His bare arms lie over his head, and his
broad chest rises and falls in the tranquil rhythm of his breathing.*

Street outside Rubini house. Dawn.

The front door opens. Sandra comes out furtively, holding the child in her arms, wrapped in a blanket.

SPEAKER: That morning Sandra left the house at dawn without a word to anyone ...

She looks up and down the deserted street, then walks quickly along the wall. A street-sweeper is cleaning the street in the chilly air. Sandra disappears into a side street.

SPEAKER: ... and at noon she had not yet returned.

Piazza with fountain. Day.

Leopoldo and Fausto are waiting by the fountain as a car approaches.

LEOPOLDO: Here's Riccardo with his father's car.

The car stops at the fountain.

LEOPOLDO: Hi, Riccardo. Hi, Alberto. *(Greetings.)* Come on, Fausto. Get in.

Inside the car. Day.

The car stops. Leopoldo and Fausto come up and get in. Fausto is tense and worried, although he tries to hide it. Alberto makes room for him.

RICCARDO *(to Fausto):* Moraldo's gone to see Mrs. Rossi, Sandra's teacher ... at school ... She might have gone there ...

The car departs.

LEOPOLDO: Yes, that's right, Fausto. I think she might be there too.

RICCARDO: Then should we go to the school first and then to the nurse?

LEOPOLDO: Yes.

RICCARDO: But how far is it to the nurse's? Because ... for the gas ...

The car drives along. Fausto stares tensely at the road. Alberto, who has been watching him, finally decides to speak.

ALBERTO *(to Fausto):* Fausto ... what happened? Did you have a fight? Eh?

Fausto does not answer.

FAUSTO: There's Moraldo.

Moraldo is standing before the doorway of an old medieval building. Beside him is an elderly woman, dressed in black, with a coat over her shoulders.

The car pulls up in front of them.

RICCARDO: Well?

MORALDO *(serious and tense):* Nothing. She hasn't seen her.

The four friends, who had expected this answer, remain silent. The teacher peers into the car to look at Fausto.

FAUSTO: Get in, we'll go to the nurse's.

Moraldo avoids looking at Fausto.

MORALDO: Go on by yourselves ... I'm going to look on my own.

And without awaiting an answer, he walks off.

TEACHER *(anxiously):* But ... what's happened?

FAUSTO: Nothing, Ma'am.

He closes the door.

RICCARDO *(calling):* Moraldo! Moraldo!

FAUSTO *(harshly):* Let him go. Let's go, get going!

The car drives off. There is a long silence. Then Alberto, trying to maintain a serious expression, turns to Leopoldo.

ALBERTO *(softly):* Listen, Leopoldo? Before we leave town ...

LEOPOLDO: Eh?

ALBERTO: Suppose we get a bite to eat before we leave town.

Leopoldo tries to avoid what might seem improper.

LEOPOLDO: No ... afterwards. I have a feeling we'll find her at the nurse's, Fausto, you know? She must have gone there ... she's gone to show her the baby, that's what!

ALBERTO: Of course. That's what I think too. She's gone to show her the baby. *(To Fausto, after a pause)* Did you eat anything before you left the house? Nothing?

FAUSTO *(worried):* No. I'm not hungry.

ALBERTO: A little sandwich ...

FAUSTO: I'm not hungry!

ALBERTO: Nothing!

The car continues on toward the country.

A fork in the country road. Day.

The car drives toward the camera and stops. Alberto and Riccardo get out.

RICCARDO: Which way do we go?

ALBERTO *(pointing):* It must be over this way, wait and let's ask.

Leopoldo gets out and hides behind a large tree, evidently to urinate.

Fausto gets out, too, and slowly starts down one of the two roads.

Alberto picks up a clod of dirt from the edge of a ditch and hurls it against the tree behind which Leopoldo is hiding; then he pretends to be admiring the landscape.

Leopoldo appears from behind the tree, rather upset.

LEOPOLDO: What kind of a joke is that? What if you hit me?

ALBERTO *(turning a deaf ear):* Who says it was me? *(Points to Riccardo.)*

The silence of the countryside is enchanting. A little bird sings up in the branches of a tree.

(Song of bird.)

RICCARDO *(listening):* Shhh. Quiet. *(Pause)* Hear the wren?

ALBERTO *(listens, then shakes his head):* What d'you mean wren! That's a robin.

RICCARDO: What d'you mean robin ... The robin goes like this: *(Whistles.)*

ALBERTO: How does the robin go?

Riccardo whistles again.

ALBERTO: The robin goes: *(He imitates the song of the robin.)*

Riccardo nervously shrugs his shoulders, then notices that Fausto has disappeared and calls:

RICCARDO: Fausto!

Countryside. Day.

In the distance, Fausto is running along a country lane.

Farmhouse. Outside. Day.

A farmhouse with a shed sheltering a cart, various tools and an old bicycle.

Fausto runs through the doorway and disappears inside.

SPEAKER: But Sandra had not been seen at the nurse's either.

A few moments later Fausto reappears in the doorway, an appalled expression on his face. He heads for the open area outside the shed, followed by a peasant woman who is drying her eyes on her apron.

SPEAKER: Fausto begins to be frightened.

Riccardo, Leopoldo and Alberto are walking quickly down the lane, which leads from the road to the house. They see from Fausto's face that Sandra's not there.

The wet nurse, who is circling around Fausto, laments.

WET NURSE: My poor little girl! ... Poor Sandra ... Holy Virgin, help her!

FAUSTO *(to Riccardo):* We'll go back.

RICCARDO *(distressed):* The car won't start. The gas isn't getting through ... the carburetor has to be taken apart.

Fausto turns quickly toward the shed and sees the bicycle leaning against the wall.

FAUSTO *(to the nurse, decisively):* Can I take the bike?

And he takes it. Riccardo tries to persuade Fausto to wait.

WET NURSE *(still following Fausto):* Yes, my boy, take it. It's Cesare's, but he doesn't need it today. Be careful not to go too fast! But don't you boys want something to eat? A little salami ... I'll make you some eggs ...

RICCARDO *(to Fausto):* Wait ... we'll all get there at the same time ...

FAUSTO *(mounting the bicycle):* Let me go. Forgive me.

He starts pedaling but Alberto stops him.

ALBERTO: Listen, Fausto! Sandra's home. Sandra's home; I'll bet you anything she's back.

FAUSTO *(out of patience):* Let me go, get out of here.

ALBERTO: Now you're getting scared? You should have thought of that earlier!

FAUSTO *(pushing Alberto roughly out of his way and beginning to pedal):* Get out of the way, you moron. Think of your sister, who hasn't come back.

ALBERTO *(shouting after him):* What do you mean? ... You coward, you rotten pig ... you bastard ...

Pedaling rapidly, Fausto disappears at the end of the lane.

Riccardo tries to calm down Alberto.

RICCARDO: Come on, Alberto, calm down. *(Coming over to the nurse)* What were you saying about some eggs?

WET NURSE: Yes.

RICCARDO: With salami?

NURSE: Yes.

RICCARDO *(turning to Alberto, who continues to feel offended):* Alberto!

ALBERTO: Leave me alone!

RICCARDO: With salami.

ALBERTO *(interested):* With salami?

RICCARDO: Yes.

They all go back toward the farmhouse.

Street outside the Rubini home. Day.

Fausto races up on his bicycle, stops before the gate, lets the bike fall to the ground and runs up the path leading to the door.

He disappears inside.

Entrance hall, Rubini home. Day.

The front door is open. Fausto runs in, looking around for someone. The house seems deserted. He races up the stairs.

FAUSTO *(calling):* Sandra!

Sandra's and Fausto's bedroom. Day.

Inside the room, the double bed and the baby's crib are unmade. The maid is sitting on the bed crying.

Fausto rushes in all disheveled.

FAUSTO *(rapidly, desperately):* What? There's nobody home?

MAID *(weeping):* They've gone to the police ... They're looking for her down at the sea.

FAUSTO *(horrified):* At the sea? Why at the sea? Why at the sea?

MAID *(weeping):* How should I know?

Fausto runs downstairs as the maid, still weeping, calls after him.

MAID: What should I do? Should I fix lunch for you?

Fausto, in anguish, does not answer.

Seashore drive. Day.

Fausto walks slowly along, pushing the bicycle and scanning the sea, thoroughly disheartened.

He stops near a café and looks around. At one of the tables sits the lady from the movie theater, who calls invitingly to him.

LADY: Oh, it's you! *(coyly)* You see, we did meet after all!

Fausto gazes at her in a daze.

FAUSTO *(tonelessly):* Eh?

LADY: Oh, what have you been up to, going around with such a long beard. Destiny! Where are you rushing to? To the movies?

FAUSTO *(murmuring):* No.

LADY *(significantly):* I'm going home ... Would you like to come along? *(Showing a package)* Would you carry this for me?

FAUSTO *(looking at the lady, still in a daze):* No, I'm sorry. No, Ma'am. I really can't, I have to go.

He turns and goes off, pushing the bicycle.

Beach. Day.

The beach, with the shacks and the pier in the background. Fausto looks about, hoping to see someone, but the beach is deserted, except for a line of little seminary students who are running along the shore, accompanied by two priests.

Fausto turns back, ever more bewildered and desperate.

Street outside Rubini house. Day.

Fausto rides up on his bicycle, gets off, and pushes the bike down the garden path. He meets Moraldo at the front door. The two stare lengthily at each other. Fausto is overcome; at first he does not dare to ask, but then decides to.

FAUSTO *(softly):* Is she back?

Moraldo shakes his head and indicates that he wants to pass by. Fausto leans up against the door.

FAUSTO *(softly):* If she doesn't come back I'll kill myself ...

MORALDO *(darting him a scornful glance):* You? You won't kill yourself. You're a coward ...

And pushing Fausto roughly away, he goes out toward the street.

Street outside religious articles store. Dusk.

Fausto walks along like a drunk. He passes in front of the display window of Michele's store.

He looks at the store, then pushes open the door and enters.

Michele rises in surprise and remains standing at his counter.

No one else is in the store.

FAUSTO *(approaching Michele):* Mr. Conti ...

He would like to go on, but a sudden overpowering sob racks his chest. He bows his head and begins to weep.

MICHELE: What's the matter?
FAUSTO *(sobbing):* Sandra's gone.

Country road. Dusk.

Riccardo, Leopoldo and Alberto are driving back to town, excited, merry, and somewhat dazed by the sun and by the wine they have consumed. Alberto is standing with his head stuck out of the open top of the car.

Some laborers are repairing the road. As the car passes them, Alberto shouts.

ALBERTO: Workers! Here!

He continues to curse and shout at them.

The workmen immediately stop their labors and exchange some indignant comments.

Alberto's voice can again be heard.

ALBERTO: Workers! Out on the rock pile!

The laborers watch the car, which has already gone another hundred yards down the road.

Inside the car on the country road. Dusk.

Leopoldo and Alberto sing.

The car begins to jerk and comes to a stop. Riccardo immediately appears worried.

RICCARDO: What the hell's the matter with this car?

ALBERTO *(worried):* What's happened? You stopping?

Alberto glances back.

RICCARDO: Get out and open the hood.

ALBERTO: Do something!

RICCARDO: What do you want me to do?

Alberto jumps out, goes to open the hood and turns to look back.

The group of laborers is standing still watching to see whether or not the car will start.

Alberto becomes impatient. Instead of opening the hood, he takes a couple of steps back.

ALBERTO *(shouting):* They're coming!

He runs off along the road and then heads into the fields.

As if released by his shout, the small band of laborers has begun running toward the car. Each of the men is carrying a tool; they yell like wild Indians.

The laborers scream.

Riccardo turns and he, too, jumps out of the car and races after Alberto

Leopoldo, who only now realizes what's happening, opens the car door instead of jumping out. The younger workmen are almost upon him. Leopoldo realizes that he will be caught if he runs, and before the attackers arrive, he points to Alberto and Riccardo who are fleeing across the fields.

LEOPOLDO: There they are ... They've gone that way!

Two of the workmen grab him and shake him.

LABORER: Now let's hear you make fun of us!

LEOPOLDO *(terrified):* I'd never think of it. I ... I didn't have anything to do with it ... *(With a weak, cowardly smile)* I'm a Socialist ...

Leopoldo manages to escape, pursued by one of the workmen.

The laborers run off shouting.

Other workmen start chasing Riccardo and Alberto.

Street outside Fausto's father's home. Night.

Fausto's little sister stands outside the open door, looking up and down as if awaiting someone. Now she looks more attentively, her face lights up and she runs toward Fausto and Michele, who are walking up the street. Fausto looks like a limp dishrag, and he drags his feet along as he exhaustedly follows Michele.

LITTLE SISTER *(calling):* Fausto! You looking for Sandra? She's here with us! Come on!

A tremulous smile appears on Fausto's face, and he throws a dazed glance at Michele. Then he suddenly starts to run toward the house. He plunges through the door and enters the pantry.

FAUSTO *(shouting):* Sandra!

Pantry. Night.

Sandra is sitting at the rear of the room, with the baby in her arms. She is pale and her eyes are swollen from weeping.

Fausto remains immobilized in the doorway for a moment. Then he starts to rush over to her with a relieved, touched smile, but his father suddenly blocks his path.

FAUSTO: Sandra!

FATHER: Stop right there. *(To Sandra)* Sandra, do me a favor. Go in there with the baby.

The father accompanies the reluctant Sandra into the next room, along with his own little daughter.

LITTLE SISTER *(imploring):* Papa, let me stay here!

He calmly closes the door and takes off his jacket.

FAUSTO *(cowardly):* Papa, if you only knew what a day this has been!

The father does not answer. He pulls the belt from his pants and approaches Fausto, who watches him perplexedly and backs slowly away.

FAUSTO *(with tears in his voice):* But Papa, what are you going to do?

The father falls on him, brandishing the belt.

In the next room, Sandra, Michele and the little sister hear Fausto's imploring shrieks as he is whipped.

Sandra is horrified.

SANDRA: Oh my God, don't you hear him!

MICHELE *(lying):* No, I don't hear anything.

SANDRA: But he's beating him! Let me go! Let me go!

MICHELE: No, they're having some argument. They're rather loud, but it's between men.

Sandra continues to protest excitedly as Michele holds her back.

Fausto appears in the doorway for a moment in an attempt to escape, but Michele pushes him back inside and closes the door again.

The father continues to hit Fausto, who, pleading, tries in vain to defend himself.

FAUSTO: No, Papa, no!!

Sandra is increasingly worried and horrified by Fausto's shrieks.

The little sister laughs, amused by the ruckus.

Fausto has caught up a chair and tries to shield himself with it from the father's blows. But the father pulls it away from him and continues his punishment.

FAUSTO: Please, Papa, no!

Michele, obviously pleased by the lesson Fausto is receiving, continues to dissuade Sandra from running to defend her husband.

SANDRA: But he's killing him!

MICHELE: No, no, he's not hurting him ... Actually ... I should think just the opposite ... *(To the screaming child)* Oh, poor little thing, poor little thing ...

Sandra can stand it no longer and dumps the baby in Michele's arms.

SANDRA: Listen, please, hold the baby for me a minute.

She runs shouting into the pantry and pulls her father-in-law off

Fausto, who is down on the floor. Then she sits down beside her husband and the two embrace.

SANDRA *(shouting):* Enough, Papa. It's enough, it's enough ...

Panting and dazed, Fausto's father comes toward Michele, who has appeared in the doorway with the child in his arms, and introduces himself as if nothing had happened.

MICHELE: May I? I'm Michele Conti. *(Then, glancing sidelong at Fausto and Sandra)* It's a very great pleasure ...

Fausto and Sandra mingle their tears as they embrace.

FAUSTO *(weeping):* You gave me such a scare!

SANDRA: Did he hurt you much, Fausto?

FAUSTO: No, no ... how are you?

Street outside Fausto's father's house. Night.

The front door opens and Fausto, carrying the baby, comes out with Sandra.

The father and the little sister wave goodbye from the doorway.

Sandra and Fausto go off down the street, turning now and then to wave.

Fausto has a black eye and a band-aid on his cheek.

FAUSTO: You made me feel so awful, Sandra. I'll never do it again!

SANDRA *(severe):* What about you? If you get me mad another time ... I'll do just like your father ... Even worse!

Fausto stops and smiles at her. For the first time he sees Sandra in a new light. She is no longer the little girl who suffered every wrong, submissive and humble, playing the role of the victim.

SANDRA *(decidedly):* I'll beat hell out of you!

Fausto looks at her again.

FAUSTO *(smiling):* That's the way I like you! Give me the baby. *(He takes the baby in his arms. He looks up at Mirella in the window.)* So long, Mirella, goodbye.

SANDRA: 'Bye, Mirella.

Fausto and Sandra go off down the street.

SPEAKER: The story of Fausto and Sandra ends here, for now. As for that of Leopoldo, of Alberto, of Riccardo, of all of us, you can imagine for yourselves. We were always talking about leaving, but one of us, one morning, without a word to anybody, did leave.

Station platform. Dawn.

(A bell rings to announce the arrival of the train.)

Moraldo stands on the platform with a suitcase in his hand, his collar up, his head bare.

(The bell stops ringing.)

A sudden silence. Moraldo looks down the track where the train is coming in rapidly and silently.

The train enters the station and stops. Moraldo opens a door in a third-class car and starts to climb up. Just then he hears someone calling him.

VOICE OF LITTLE RAILROAD BOY: Moraldo! Moraldo! Moraldo!

He turns and finds the little boy standing beside him, his sharp-witted little face gazing at him in surprise under a dirty cap.

(Train whistles.)

BOY: Where are you going, you leaving?

MORALDO: Guido. Yes, I'm leaving.

BOY: Where are you going!

MORALDO *(evasive):* I don't know. I'm leaving. I don't know.

Moraldo climbs into the train. The conductor walks along the cars slamming the doors.

CONDUCTOR *(shouting):* All aboard! All aboard!

The boy remains beside the closed door, with an incredulous smile on his funny little face.

Moraldo stands at the window. The train starts to pull out. The boy, fascinated by Moraldo, follows the train.

BOY: Then what are you going to do?

MORALDO: I don't know! I have to leave. I'm going away.

BOY: But weren't you happy here?

Moraldo does not answer.

BOY: So long, Moraldo! So long, goodbye!

MORALDO *(touched):* Goodbye, Guido!

BOY *(from a distance):* 'Bye! ...

The boy stops and waves with an uncertain smile. The train picks up speed.

On the train. Dawn.

Moraldo leans against the window and watches the station buildings parading past him, the iron bridge over which the train rumbles, the houses of the silent white city in the uncertain light of dawn.

A shadow of deep melancholy darkens Moraldo's face.

Four rapidly juxtaposed shots show, sleeping in their respective beds...

Leopoldo's room. Dawn.

Leopoldo sleeps with a book open on the pillow; the lamp is still lit.

(Sound of train.)

Riccardo's room. Dawn.

Riccardo sleeps embracing his pillow.

(Sound of train.)

Alberto's room. Dawn.

Alberto snores heavily in his bed.

(Sound of train.)

Sandra's and Fausto's room. Dawn.

Sandra and Fausto sleep with the baby between them.

(Sound of train.)

On the train. Dawn.

Moraldo watches the last house on the outskirts of town disappear in the brightening morning light. He leans out one last time, extending his hand in a vague wave.

Station platform. Dawn.

The train is disappearing on the horizon. The little railway boy turns with a pirouette and, whistling merrily, picks up his lamp, hops onto the rail and goes off playing the tightrope walker.

The End

Il Bidone

Credits

Plot and screenplay:	Federico Fellini
	Ennio Flaiano
	Tullio Pinelli
Director of photography:	Otello Martelli (A.I.C.)
Production director:	Giuseppe Colizzi (A.D.C.)
Editing:	Mario Serandrei
	Giuseppe Vari
Artistic collaborator:	Brunello Rondi
Sets and costumes:	Dario Cecchi
Director's Aides:	Moraldo Rossi
	Narciso Vicario
Assistant directors:	Dominique Delouche
	Paolo Nuzzi
Editing secretary:	Nada Delle Piane
Make-up:	Eligio Trani
Hair stylist:	Fiamma Rocchetti
Set photographer:	G. B. Poletto
Decorator:	Massimiliano Capriccioli
Sound technician:	Giovanni Rossi
Cameraman:	Roberto Gerardi (A.I.C.)
Assistant cameraman:	Arturo Zavattini (A.I.C.)
Production inspector:	Antonio Negri
Production secretary:	Manolo Bolognini
Administrative secretary:	Ezio Rodi

Music: Nino Rota
Conducted by: Franco Ferrara
"TITANUS" musical editions
Director: Federico Fellini
An Italo-French co-production
"TITANUS" — S.G.C.
The film was produced using the facilities of "TITANUS"
Negative KODAK
Development and Printing
STACO FILM
Sound recording on R.C.A. equipment
All reference to persons, events, and places are purely coincidental.

Cast:

Broderick Crawford
Giulietta Masina
Richard Basehart
Franco Fabrizi
Sue Ellen Blake
Alberto de Amicis
Giacomo Gabrielli
Irene Cefaro
Lorella de Luca
Riccardo Garrone
Paul Grenter

Country road. Day.

A lonely country road winding up a hill through deserted fields and patches of scrub.

A man is seated beneath a tree in the midst of this silent, lonely setting. He is a short fellow, dressed with a sort of specious chic; his hawk-like face is deeply marked, and his eyes are cold and lucid. He is studying a racing sheet and occasionally pencils notes in the margins.

A shiny black limousine drives down the opposite side of the road.

The man ("Baron" Vargas) raises his head and looks toward the road.

Vargas rises, picks up the briefcase and raincoat he has propped against a tree and walks toward the car, which has stopped near a little bridge.

The driver gets out of the car. He is a well-built, self-assured young Roman whose apparent cordiality masks an extremely cynical and calculating nature.

The young man (Roberto) wears a black chauffeur's uniform. He calls to Vargas as he gets out of the car.

ROBERTO: Hi there, old man! Our dear Baron!

VARGAS: Look, it's ten-thirty; do I always have to wait for you?

Roberto addresses a sort of bass yodel toward the countryside and immediately goes to open the trunk of the car.

Vargas opens the rear door. Two men are in the back seat, with the collars of their overcoats pulled up.

One of them (Augusto) is a man of about fifty. His features are harsh and his cheeks hollow; his eyes are heavy and melancholy but always alert, and his smile sometimes twists into an ironical grimace. The other man (Picasso) is fair with light blue eyes; he is thirty but seems younger. He gives the impression of being both sly and innocent at the same time.

Vargas is obviously angered.

VARGAS *(calmly but severely):* What've you been up to? Where were you?

Augusto, who seems quite vexed, does not even bother to answer, and simply shrugs his shoulders.

PICASSO *(laughing softly, pointing to Roberto):* We lost Roberto this morning. *(Laughs.)* That guy's got a woman in every village.

Picasso gets out of the car; he is wearing a priest's cassock under his Montgomery coat.

Behind the car, Roberto hums and chuckles as he substitutes a fake Vatican license plate for the one that belongs to the car.

PICASSO *(looking about, exclaims joyfully):* Hey, look how beautiful it is out here!

Vargas shows a map to Augusto, who is still inside the car.

VARGAS *(protesting):* It's only ten kilometers. You could've been there by now. *(Augusto gets out and goes to the rear of the car.)* Why do we always have to screw things up?

Picasso goes toward the bridge, hopping to warm up; he bends over the side to look at the gully beneath.

PICASSO: Looks like a Corot landscape, doesn't it?

Augusto carefully folds his coat and deposits it in the trunk, from which Roberto is removing some equipment. He hands Augusto a red cardinal's ribbon.

ROBERTO *(calmly, holding the red ribbon out to Augusto):* Here ...
     Go hang yourself ...

*Augusto begins to wrap the ribbon about himself. Vargas, mean-
while, has taken a sheet of paper from his briefcase and slowly walks
with Augusto over to Picasso, who is sitting on the railing of the
bridge.*

VARGAS *(to Picasso):* Look, here's the map ... That mark there is the
     tree. Eight paces from the tree is the treasure.

PICASSO: Hm ... hm hm ... I get it ...

VARGAS *(pointing to Picasso's shoes):* What d'you think you're doing
     with yellow shoes?

PICASSO *(somewhat humiliated):* You can't see them under the
     cassock ...

He begins to take off his coat.

AUGUSTO: Give me that cross, will you?

*Picasso extracts from his pocket a large pectoral cross and chain,
which appears to be gold, and tosses them to Augusto, who hangs the
cross around his neck.*

PICASSO: Here! *(Then he turns to Vargas, indicating a point on the
     sketch map)* And these numbers?

VARGAS: Five feet down. Understand? The ground on top has been
     fixed up like it was before and you can't tell at all. You just
     dig. I think that we can wind everything up before night. *(He
     comes over to Augusto and, indicating Roberto.)* Oh ... Tell
     that moron to stop trying to be so funny, 'cause the women
     aren't that dumb ...

*Roberto, screwing on the license plate, whistles mockingly at
Vargas.*

VARGAS: Oh, one more thing, I forgot. Be careful, there are a couple of nasty dogs. *(Looking at Augusto's hands)* Where's the ring?

AUGUSTO *(annoyed):* I've got it, I 've got it ...

VARGAS: Hey, what's got into you this morning? Eh? You nervous? *(Without awaiting an answer, Vargas approaches Roberto, who has finished changing the license plate)* Let me have a

look. Everything set here? *(Softly, indicating Augusto)* Hey, what's got into Augusto this morning?

ROBERTO: He's on his last legs, the old man. He's about to drop dead.

Augusto completes his costume.

PICASSO *(smiling and indicating the countryside):* Augusto ... nice spot, isn't it?

Frowning, Augusto nods. Then he takes the ring from his pocket and puts it on his finger.

Before closing the trunk, Roberto takes out two priest's hats; he whistles to Augusto and Picasso as he tosses them the hats.

Augusto and Picasso catch their hats on the fly and put them on; Augusto's has a ribbon on it.

ROBERTO *(announcing):* All aboard! On the road!

He opens the rear door and Augusto and Picasso climb back in.

Valley with farm. Day.

The car drives rapidly down a dusty road.

Farm. Day.

The car drives up to a large farmhouse. Two huge watchdogs bark ferociously, racing around the car as it comes up the lane and stops in the farmyard.

No one gets out of the car.

Inside the car, Roberto eggs on the dogs, amused and excited by their barking.

ROBERTO: Aah ... aaah ... *(Laughs.)* Boo ... boo ...

No one appears. The dogs continue to bark furiously, circling around the car.

Someone is observing the visitors from behind the half-closed door of the barn. It is an elderly woman, big-boned and strong, whose tiny eyes stare suspiciously out of her masculine face.

Picasso is the first to notice her.

PICASSO: Oh, good morning, Ma'am. Good morning. Please excuse us. Would you mind calling off the dogs, please?

The woman finally decides to open the barn door and directs some gutteral shouts at the dogs.

A moment of silence. Roberto, who has gotten out of the car, comes toward her.

ROBERTO *(loudly):* Does Stella Fiorina live here? *(The woman comes a few steps forward but does not answer.)* Is Stella Fiorina here? Hm?

WOMAN *(hostile, suspicious):* What do you want? ... I'm Stella Fiorina!

ROBERTO *(elegantly removing his cap and turning to Augusto):* Monsignor, it's her.

Picasso has opened the rear door and gotten out quickly.

Meanwhile, a second woman has appeared from behind the house; she is smaller than the first, and at once curious and frightened.

Picasso greets her; then, with exaggerated unctuousness and a certain apprehension for the dogs, he comes toward the first woman, holding a leather briefcase under his arm.

PICASSO: Ah, good morning ... *Pax et bonum!* It's a great pleasure, Mrs. Stella Fiorina. You are the proprietor of this farm, I believe, aren't you? We have something extremely private to talk to you about. His Eminence has sent his Referendarium, Monsignor De Filippis, on purpose from Rome ...

So saying, Picasso turns and bows slightly toward the car, where Augusto is majestically getting out, with the obsequious assistance of

Roberto. The two old ladies exchange glances. The second, hastily straightening her apron, runs toward Augusto, curtsies awkwardly and kisses his ring.

SECOND WOMAN: Oh, Monsignor!

Augusto makes the gesture of benediction. Then he moves toward the first old lady, who is standing there, immobile and stiff.

AUGUSTO *(softly):* We want to talk with you ... privately. Is that possible?

Suspicious and somewhat fearful, the woman starts slowly for the house, followed by Augusto, Picasso and Roberto.

Farmhouse kitchen. Day.

The first woman ushers in Augusto and the others, saying reverently:

FIRST WOMAN: Come in ... Excuse me if it's dirty here. *(She shoos a little country girl, who is holding a dirty baby in her arms, out of the room.)* Get out. Excuse me, Monsignor. *(To the girl)* Get out, get out.

PICASSO *(to the baby):* Cute little kid!

The old woman, still somewhat frightened, approaches the rough table, where Augusto and Picasso are standing, and stares harshly at them.

AUGUSTO *(softly to Picasso):* Don Pietro, would you please close the door?

Picasso silently closes the door and returns to the table. In the silence, Augusto motions to him to open the briefcase. Picasso quickly and obsequiously removes some papers from it and lays them out on the table.

The two women follow his movements with growing apprehension.

Augusto begins in a low, mysterious voice, occasionally half-closing his eyes and circling slowly around the table.

AUGUSTO: On the point of death, a poor sinner decided to confide a terrible, terrible secret ... It was a question of murder ... *(He stops for a lengthy pause and sighs deeply, his eyes half closed.)* During the war, when the front passed through these parts, the deceased man was fleeing with an accomplice after having committed a theft somewhere. He killed his partner and hid the corpse in a place which, according to what he told us, should be on your property ...

Extremely astonished, the two old women exchange a bewildered glance. Picasso exploits the pause.

PICASSO *(holding out the sketch map):* Excuse me, but do you have on your farm here a tree standing in the middle of a field all by itself?

FIRST WOMAN *(astonished):* Yes, behind the vineyard ...

AUGUSTO *(softly and gravely):* That's it ... *(Another pause)* Well, it is my duty to gather up the poor remains, to bury them again in consecrated ground ... It is a holy work which you must help me do for the peace of the murderer's soul ... *(Brief pause)* Is it far from here? ...

SECOND WOMAN: No ... it's past the vineyard ...

FIRST WOMAN *(alarmed, still not having well understood):* But what do you want to do? ...

AUGUSTO: Tell me, is this a fairly tranquil place? I mean, there's no danger of being seen? Because I would prefer not to wait for night. All the more so because it won't take much time and actually we wouldn't even need your help.

Picasso pretends to suggest something quietly to Augusto.

PICASSO: The treasure ... *(He approaches Augusto and repeats)* The treasure ...

Augusto smiles, deprecating his forgetfulness, and continues:

AUGUSTO: Oh yes, yes, I'd forgotten. It seems that along with the remains there are some jewels that the two men had stolen. Perhaps the murderer was planning to come back and take them at some later date. Actually, it's a little treasure. The Father has the letter here ... *(Pointing to the briefcase)* But this is of no importance to us. Because the deceased man expressly declared that if it is found, it shall remain the property of the owner of the land; that is, you ... With the exception, as he said, of whatever is necessary for some Masses for the salvation of his soul. *(He gazes most gravely at the two women.)* You will promise to keep this secret, of course? In your own interest, too, because the Government might, unlawfully, advance some claim.

FIRST WOMAN *(amazed):* A treasure?

AUGUSTO *(very gently):* Yes, but for us the important thing is to bury the poor remains.

Field with tree. Day.

A tree stands alone in a deserted field. The first old woman looks about, suspicious and diffident.

Augusto, Picasso and Roberto are standing near the tree. Roberto is carrying a spade.

Picasso and Augusto are consulting the map; Picasso indicates the various reference points: the well, the tree, the vineyard.

PICASSO: Here's the tree. Eight paces from this point toward the vineyard ... If you'll allow me, Monsignor, I'd like to try to pace them off.

WOMAN *(to Roberto):* Here. *(Roberto nods.)*

PICASSO: Excuse me, Monsignor ... Excuse me a minute ... *(He measures eight long paces from the well toward the tree.)* One, two, three, four, five, six, seven and eight ... *(Repeats.)* eight. *(He stops and, with macabre solemnity, indicates the spot to Augusto.)* Monsignor, it should be here. In exactly this spot here.

The two women watch attentively.

AUGUSTO *(softly):* Well, shall we try? *(Looking at the two women)* You're agreed, aren't you?

The two women nod.

AUGUSTO *(to Roberto):* Would you mind starting, Roberto?

ROBERTO: As you say, Monsignor.

Roberto hands his cap to the old woman, comes over to Picasso and drives the spade into the ground.

ROBERTO: Look out!!

He takes off his jacket and hands it to the second woman; he gives his glasses to the first woman, saying jokingly in English:

ROBERTO: Please ...

Picasso leads the second woman to one side as Roberto begins to dig.

PICASSO: Come, Ma'am. Come stand a little further over here.

Half an hour later, Roberto is up to his knees in the hole he has dug. The two old women watch him from nearby; Augusto and Picasso are standing somewhat further off in the field.

Panting with his efforts, Roberto stops digging.

ROBERTO *(to himself):* I'm worn out ... *(Calling to Augusto)* Monsignor, there's nothing down here. I'm going to rest a little.

So saying, he climbs out of the hole, hands the spade to the first old woman and goes toward Augusto and Picasso

FIRST WOMAN: Give it to me.

She climbs down into the hole and begins to dig with peasant energy.

The second old woman watches her sister's labors anxiously from the edge of the hole. For a short while the only sound is the clang of iron on dirt.

SECOND WOMAN: Be careful, Stella.

Suddenly the old women emit a choked exclamation of astonishment and fear, and stare at something in the ground.

FIRST WOMAN: Monsignor, come here!

PICASSO *(looking over at the two women):* Augusto, here we are!

The three men run toward the old women and stop at the edge of the hole.

FIRST WOMAN: Monsignor, look!

ROBERTO: My God, he was right.

Augusto nods silently and gravely.

AUGUSTO: Poor soul! ...

Roberto leaps into the hole and bends over to pick up a white skull.

PICASSO *(calmly):* Careful, careful, give it to me, Roberto ... There, that's it, thanks...

Roberto hands the skull to Picasso, who receives it with a great show of reverence.

The second woman makes the sign of the cross and begins to mumble prayers.

SECOND WOMAN: *Requiem aeternam dona eius Domine ...*

Picasso opens a large silk cloth, lays it out on the ground and places the skull on it.

PICASSO *(to himself):* This is what we've come to! Oh dear Lord!

Roberto digs around in the bottom of the hole and pulls out more bones.

ROBERTO: Look what a pile of bones! And look at the size of this one!

The first old woman suddenly falls down on hands and knees and gropes around the bottom of the hole with her hands.

FIRST WOMAN: There's something here. There's something.

Augusto mumbles some Latin words, with a broad gesture of benediction.

AUGUSTO: *Requiem aeternam dona eius Domine.*

FIRST WOMAN: Monsignor!

Sweating and panting with her exertions, the first woman is digging up a little metal casket fastened with a chain; she finally pulls it out of the ground and holds it up.

FIRST WOMAN: Look, Monsignor! Here it is!

ROBERTO: Ah, Monsignor, here it is.

Farmhouse kitchen. Day.

The casket stands open on the table. The cloth with the bones has been set down on a chair.

A large number of precious objects glitter inside the casket: necklaces, bracelets, rings, etc. Picasso, sitting at the table, lifts them out one by one, checking them against a list.

PICASSO *(murmuring apparently to himself)*: One necklace with diamond and rubies ... A bar of gold weighing ... two kilos ... here it is ... Then, an intarsia gold pin ...

Augusto, sitting a little further off, drinks down a glass of sweet liqueur and pours himself another. Roberto is standing up, eating some eggs with obvious appetite.

A huge fire is burning in the fireplace; its reflections gleam on the jewels lined up on the table.

The two old women stare at the gold and gems in fascination; they appear to be in a state of great inner turmoil.

FIRST WOMAN *(holding her breath)*: But is it all good stuff? ...

ROBERTO *(ostensibly childish)*: I'd like to get *my* hands on it ... *(He pretends to catch himself up and excuse himself to Monsignor)* No, Monsignor ... I meant that if it wasn't real gold, after so many years buried in the ground, by now it would be all black ...

PICASSO: Well, I think it might be about five or six million lire ...

SECOND WOMAN: How much did you say?

PICASSO *(artfully changing the subject):* Excuse me, could I have a glass of water?

SECOND WOMAN *(softly, to her sister):* Six million.

She goes to get him a drink.

PICASSO: Um, yes. About six million. Well, more or less, about that amount.

ROBERTO: It must be more. At the price of gold today, Father. It's gone up, you know.

PICASSO: Oh, you must be right ... it would be more. It must be more. It must be around seven million.

ROBERTO *(trying the necklace on the old woman):* Let's see how it looks ...

SECOND WOMAN: What do we have to do? We have to split it with you?

PICASSO *(to reassure them, softly):* No, no, no. Of course not ... absolutely not ... It's yours. It's all yours.

Augusto takes a sheet of paper from the briefcase, shows it to Picasso and begins to read.

AUGUSTO: If I may ... *(Reading)* "To whom it may concern: In atrocious remorse for the evil I have committed, and with the terror of having to pay for my sins among the eternal flames of Hell, I hereby order that all the wealth criminally acquired by me and buried beside the corpse of my victim shall, since its legitimate owners are now dead, become the property of the owners of the land on which they are to be found, with one condition only" ... *(He stops and solemnly indicates the paper.)* I'm reading from the original manuscript. *(Reading again)* "... with one condition only: that the owners of the

land shall have five hundred Masses said for the salvation of my soul..."

He closes his eyes with a great melancholy sigh.

The two women look at each other, half-worried and half-reassured.

FIRST WOMAN: We're supposed to pay for the Masses?

SECOND WOMAN: We should have our own parish priest say them? ...

Augusto gently gestures no.

AUGUSTO *(paternally):* No, no, no ... I'll have them sung in Saint Peter's ... It will be much better that way.

PICASSO *(smiling discretely):* Five hundred Masses at one thousand lire each ... *(With an open smile)* Not very much at all ...

FIRST WOMAN *(practically and somewhat dismayed):* Five hundred thousand ...

Augusto begins to read from the paper again.

AUGUSTO *(reading):* "Should the owners of the land refuse this ill-gotten gold, I beseech His Eminence to distribute it to the poor ..."

Roberto has stopped chewing and Picasso can barely hide his nervousness. This is the decisive moment. The two women look at the gold. They look at each other. The first old woman tries one last defense:

FIRST WOMAN: We have to pay for them all together?

PICASSO: That's what's written here ...

Augusto spreads wide his arms and nods gently. Then, with mysterious severity, as if the woman had already accepted, he adds:

AUGUSTO: And always remember that it is an extremely serious secret ... There's a murder involved here ... you might even become implicated yourselves. *(Emphatically)* You must never speak of it to anyone.

The two women, frightened, nod yes.

The first woman is somewhat alarmed at the thought of having to pay all that money.

FIRST WOMAN: We don't have enough to pay all of it at once ...

The second woman whispers rapidly to her.

SECOND WOMAN: We'll sell the cows.

FIRST WOMAN *(curtly, softly):* Keep quiet ...

SECOND WOMAN: We can do it.

The three men have exchanged a rapid glance. They wait for a moment, then Picasso breaks the silence.

PICASSO *(discretely):* Well ... Monsignor, we could take the gold bar ... it certainly must be worth more, no? ... this must be worth at least a million and a half, wouldn't you say?

AUGUSTO *(firmly):* No, no, absolutely no. We'll have to find some other way. In the meantime, look, Don Pietro, you take it all and we'll bring it to His Eminence in Rome. You can be quite sure he'll find a solution. Well, shall we go?

PICASSO: Certainly, Monsignor ... certainly.

And Picasso starts to gather up the jewels and close the casket.

The faces of the two women express sudden anxiety; they consult each other mutely.

FIRST WOMAN: Monsignor, excuse me. Could you wait just a minute? I want to talk to my sister.

Picasso puts the casket back on the table as the two old women go out, conversing softly.

The three men watch them anxiously.

Farmyard. Late afternoon.

The day is drawing to a close. The cows pass through the silent farmyard on their way to the barn, occasionally mooing.

Farmhouse kitchen. Late afternoon.

The kitchen is immersed in shadows. Augusto is still sitting at the table drinking. The bottle is half-empty by now. Picasso paces nervously up and down, squeezing his hands together.

Roberto, sitting backwards on a chair, rocks back and forth as he taps a cowbell. There is an atmosphere of tension, which each of the three men tries to hide in his own way.

PICASSO: Roberto, will you cut that out, please, huh?

At last Picasso stops and looks at his watch. He is alarmed.

PICASSO: Oh, it's already five o'clock. We better cut out of here.

He turns to the others and starts to add something when the door opens. The three men turn to look.

The little girl enters the kitchen with the baby in her arms.

PICASSO: Oh here they are now. *(To the baby)* Hi, little cutie. Oh, you look like a real little rascal, you know? *(To the girl)* Say ... where did the ladies go, anyway?

GIRL *(like a wild animal):* They went to town with the cart.

She goes out, closing the door behind her.

Picasso looks at the other men, puzzled and a little alarmed.

PICASSO *(softly):* To town? What did they go to town for? ...

Roberto laughs softly.

ROBERTO *(cruelly, as if quoting a newspaper headline):* "False Monsignor, fifty years old, jailed ..."

Piazza del Popolo, Rome. Night.

The car is parked in Piazza del Popolo in Rome. Picasso gets out and hurriedly says goodbye to Augusto and Roberto

PICASSO: So long ... Augusto.

AUGUSTO: So long ...

Roberto slams the door shut and the car drives off.

Picasso, who is carrying a package, starts up Via del Babuino.

Stairway leading to Picasso's apartment. Night.

Picasso takes the stairs two by two, softly whistling a conventional signal, toward the upper floors of the ramshackle building in this artists' quarter of the city.

PICASSO *(whistles a conventional signal. Then he shouts upstairs):*
Iris ... Iris ...

His wife Iris appears on one of the upstairs landings; she is a young woman with an almost perpetually frightened look on her face. She shouts back, happily surprised but with a slight note of worry:

IRIS: Carlo ...

PICASSO *(shouting from downstairs):* Hi! Get the baby dressed and come on down! ... We're going to eat out ... and then to the movies! ...

IRIS: But we were already eating! ...

PICASSO: No, we're going out. Hurry up.

IRIS: All right.

And despite her objections, Iris goes joyfully back to their apartment.

A door on the top floor opens revealing a child of about five (Silvana).

SILVANA: Papa! ... Papa! ... Hi, Papa! ... Hi, Papa!

PICASSO: Sweetheart, come on down to Papa.

Meanwhile, in the kitchen, Iris removes the pot from the stove and throws its contents into the garbage can.

The little girl runs down the stairs and meets Picasso half-way. She throws herself into his arms; he lifts her up and kisses her joyfully.

SILVANA: Hi, Papa.

Picasso carries the child slowly up the stairs and talks in a comically serious tone of voice between one kiss and another.

PICASSO: Here's my little monkey.

SILVANA: Where were you, Papa?

PICASSO: Hug your Papa tight. Listen, yesterday a lady in Viterbo asked me: Do you know a little girl in Rome that's called Silvana?

SILVANA: Me, me, me.

So saying, Picasso shows her a little purse which he has taken out of the package. Silvana begins to scream joyfully and impatiently, trying to grab it. She catches it and smothers her father with kisses.

PICASSO: Here ...

SILVANA: Ah, a pocketbook for me.

PICASSO: Yes, my love ... How many kisses for her Papa. Listen, now go call Mama, eh? Tell her to come right away.

He sets her down and the child runs up the rest of the stairs.

Picasso's home. Night.

Silvana runs in carrying the pocketbook.

SILVANA: Mama! ... Look what Papa brought me. He said a lady in Viterbo gave it to him. But I don't believe him.

IRIS: Ooh! ... Yes, but now get dressed quickly, we're going out to eat! *(Quickly slips on the child's coat)* And what's inside the little pocketbook? *(She hands the child her bonnet.)* Put this on by yourself.

Iris puts on a Montgomery jacket and straightens her hair, using the glass pane of the door as a mirror; then she goes out with the little girl.

IRIS: Let's go ...

Stairway. Night.

As he waits, Picasso carefully unwraps a second little package and takes out a brooch. He gazes at it for some moments, but when he hears footsteps on the stairs, he puts it in his pocket.

Iris and the little girl come down to the bottom of the stairs. He comes up to them and kisses Iris, who kisses him back warmly.

IRIS: Dear, at last.

PICASSO: How are you, darling?

IRIS: But you were supposed to come back last night! ...

PICASSO: Yes, but I had to ...

IRIS: Why?

PICASSO: I'll tell you later. Look, take a look at this.

He takes the little box out of his pocket and shows the brooch to Iris.

IRIS *(pleased, astonished and a little alarmed):* Oh, is it for me? How much did it cost? ...

PICASSO: Oh, well ... tell me if you like it.

IRIS: Oh, yes, so much.

SILVANA: What is it, what is it? I want to see, Mama.

IRIS: Come look.

PICASSO: Wait, let me pin it on. *(He pins the brooch on her sweater.)*

IRIS: Where are we going to eat?

PICASSO: Wherever you want. We can decide later.

IRIS: It's magnificent. What a nice gift.

IRIS: Let's go. But you could have sent a telegram. You know how I worry.

PICASSO: I didn't think of it. No, but it wasn't ...

They walk out of the building.

IRIS: And if I need you I don't know how to get hold of you.

PICASSO: Yes, but it's not my fault ...

Via Margutta. Night.

The three walk along Via Margutta.

PICASSO *(continuing):* ... What can you expect, that's what a salesman's life is like. And anyway we sold everything, you know? ... Because there was a market near there and

Augusto said we ought to go there too ... And in fact we sold everything. And look, they even paid in cash.

He immediately takes a roll of bills from his pocket and shows them triumphantly to Iris.

IRIS *(marveling):* It's all ours?

PICASSO: Of course. Whose else?

IRIS: How much is it?

PICASSO: A hundred thousand. We ought to split it this way: give at least twenty to the restaurant. *(On second thought)* Well, even ten would do ... and then ... Oh, listen, nobody came looking for me today, did they?

IRIS: No ... no. But what have you done?

PICASSO: Well, we sold them, didn't we? *(Much relieved, he continues his accounts.)* So, ten to the restaurant ... These ten to your mother, so she'll leave us alone ...

IRIS: No, no, we'll give twenty to the restaurant, and we'll pay the bakery too and everybody else. That way I can breathe easier for a while and I can go out without everybody staring at me that way.

Picasso approves with exaggerated energy.

PICASSO: Fine, fine, as you like. In fact, you hold onto it yourself, it's better that way.

He gives her the money.

IRIS: Oh, you'll see, I'll make it last a month. That way you can do some painting.

PICASSO *(playing with the child):* Oh, look what a pretty little face.

IRIS *(insisting):* And look, you must do some painting, you know!

PICASSO *(evasive):* Sure, of course I must ... Ah, Iris, I've seen more

landscapes! We have to go together one day, you know? Some countryside out on the hills that not even the Dutch could dream of ...

They go off arm in arm, with Picasso carrying the little girl

Grotte del Piccione cabaret. Inside. Night.

The band is playing South American music as a Negro dancer performs a wild dance on roller skates in the center of the floor.

The room is half-empty; only a few tables are occupied.

Weak applause greets the end of the dance. One man (Riccardo) sitting with a girl calls out at the Negro as he leaves the floor:

RICCARDO: God, what a bore!

Augusto and Roberto, dressed in dark suits, appear at the door and stop to look around with the air of old customers. They nod a greeting to the waiters, who do not, however, move toward them.

The musicians notice their arrival; one of them calls out in a gutteral tone, imitated by the others, and for some moments the rhythm of the music accelerates.

ROBERTO *(to the musicians):* Hey there boys!

MUSICIAN *(ironically):* Here comes the big money! ...

Augusto beckons over the cigarette man and, taking a package from the tray, tosses it to one of the musicians.

AUGUSTO: Catch!

Then he takes another, which he tosses to another musician.

AUGUSTO: Smoke!

MUSICIAN: Thanks!

Augusto pays the cigarette man, then calls the waiter over in an urbane tone of voice:

AUGUSTO: Luigi, come here a minute.

The waiter hurries over in an impeccable manner.

AUGUSTO: What's the best champagne you have?

WAITER: We have "Cordon Rouge," "Henri Jonet" ...

Augusto points to Roberto, who is stepping about to the music.

AUGUSTO: Let him choose the champagne.

ROBERTO *(laughing):* If it's up to me ... *(Pirouetting)* Henri Jonet!

Augusto is ostentatiously displaying a ten-thousand lire bill, which he gives to the waiter; he turns for a moment, then indicates the musicians.

AUGUSTO: And bring something to drink for those poor thirsty guys...

WAITER *(passes by the maître d', whispering):* Did they order?

MUSICIAN: Thanks!

ROBERTO: Here's to yours!

RICCARDO: Hey, Roberto, who have you conned today?

ROBERTO: Tsk tsk, Riccardo.

Augusto and Roberto have sat down at one of the tables.

The maître d', who has been observing, comes over and lights Augusto's cigarette.

MAITRE D' *(confidential, servile):* Everything all right, Mr. Rocca?

Augusto thanks him with a nod and the maître d' walks off.

Roberto has been glancing at a table with a group of Americans, among whom is a heavily bejeweled middle-aged woman. He glances meaningfully at Augusto, then rises, crosses the room, and goes over to the Americans' table and invites the woman to dance.

She is extremely flattered and accepts Roberto's invitation.

Riccardo and his girl also rise and begin to dance.

The waiter returns to Augusto's table with the champagne bucket.

RICCARDO: Hey, Roberto ... Roberto! Did you see the Cadillac outside? It's full of money!

Pleasantly surprised, Roberto winks at Riccardo and murmurs to the American lady.

ROBERTO: Do you like Italy? Eh?

AMERICAN LADY: Yes. Very much.

Augusto begins to sip his champagne and looks about. He sees a pretty girl in a black tutu leaning against a wall and looking insistently at him with her big blue eyes.

Augusto looks her up and down, quite unsubtly. Then, in a somewhat detached manner, he breaks the ice.

AUGUSTO: You work here?

The girl (Maggie) answers immediately with a foreign accent.

MAGGIE: Excuse me?

AUGUSTO: I said ... you dance?

MAGGIE: I do the harlequin dance.

AUGUSTO *(observing her amusedly):* What are you? ... German? ...

MAGGIE: No, I'm English.

A moment's pause. Then Augusto again turns to the girl, who is singing softly.

AUGUSTO: What, do you sing too?

MAGGIE *(shaking her head):* No. Just for myself ...

AUGUSTO: You're a beautiful-looking girl!

The girl is obviously pleased with the compliment. She turns to call another dancer.

MAGGIE: Frances!

FRANCES: Yes!

MAGGIE *(to Augusto):* I have to go. It's my number.

AUGUSTO: Fine, go, fine.

She smiles meaningfully at Augusto once more. The two girls make their entrance onto the dance floor, where they perform their number. Augusto watches Maggie with interest.

At the Americans' table, Roberto is writing down a telephone number.

ROBERTO: Fine ... Ah ... Tomorrow morning ... Ah ... I look ... Car ...

He makes the gesture of driving.

One of the Americans asks:

AMERICAN: What do you mean, a car?

ROBERTO: Automobile ... Two millions!

AMERICAN: Two millions? Oh, that's a lot. Is that your car?

ROBERTO: Yes, me, me ... Wonderful?

AMERICAN: Must be a very fine car!

Roberto kisses the American lady's hand.

The English girl continues to dance under Augusto's attentive gaze.

A few hours later. The cabaret is closing for the night. The musicians put their instruments away and start out.

Roberto amuses himself beating away at the drums.

MUSICIAN *(waving to Augusto):* Good night.

AUGUSTO: You're going to wreck the whole works there.

ROBERTO: Let me alone ... *(He continues to drum furiously, then stops and laughs coarsely.)* Listen to this, Augusto. This is for you. (He beats out a funeral march.)

Augusto turns to the waiter, who is sweeping up.

AUGUSTO *(annoyed and rather high):* Just look at the kind of idiot I have to work with. People that are just good for living off women. I have to laugh ...

WAITER: Oh, that's what youngsters are like today.

AUGUSTO: But I was never like that. I was always a very fancy worker. I've been all over the world and I always conned everybody. Because the world is full of fools. I could even sell ice to the Eskimos. But I have to work with these amateurs. But I'm going to go back to working alone.

As Augusto talks, the waiter removes his jacket and goes out.

Maggie, the English girl, reappears from the back room, already dressed and ready to leave. She comes over to Augusto.

MAGGIE: Shall we go?

Street outside the cabaret. Dawn.

The street is deserted at four in the morning; the white light of dawn distorts and discolors everything.

Roberto, Augusto, and Maggie come out of the cabaret with one of the musicians. Roberto is holding a violin; the musician protests as he tries to recover it.

MUSICIAN: Hey, gimme the violin before you break it. Don't fool around like that, you'll break it. It costs forty thousand lire, give it to me.

ROBERTO: No, I won't give it back unless you play.

He pretends to play the instrument, dancing and singing as he goes.

MUSICIAN: Come here, I'll play for you, come on.

ROBERTO: Will you play it?

MUSICIAN: I'll play it.

Roberto hands back the violin.

ROBERTO: Come on, play, let's hear you, come on.

The musician begins to play as Roberto dances around with the violin case in his arms.

Augusto is following them arm-in-arm with Maggie.

AUGUSTO *(to Maggie, pointing to Roberto):* Gook-looking kid, Roberto, isn't he? You like him?

Maggie looks kindly and warmly at him.

MAGGIE: I prefer to be with you. Don't you want to?

Roberto and the violinist continue down the middle of the street as Augusto and Maggie follow.

Café Canova, Piazza del Popolo, Rome. Day.

Augusto is talking with a tall Milanese gentleman.

He takes a tissue-paper package out of his pocket and delicately unwraps a woman's wrist watch.

AUGUSTO: But look, on my word of honor, I assure you it's a real
   bargain. I happen to be short of cash just now, really almost
   broke. I'll let you have it for fifteen thousand lire. It's my
   wife's. I gave it to her myself and believe me I wouldn't be
   selling it if ... I weren't at the end of my rope. You know,
   sometimes a person has these difficult moments ...

The Milanese takes the watch and examines it attentively. Then he shakes his head and smiles.

Roberto enters the café.

ROBERTO: Hi there! Hello. *(He sees the watch and feigns surprise.)*
   But what are you doing, you selling it?

AUGUSTO *(in bitter resignation):* Yes . . .

ROBERTO: For how much?

AUGUSTO: For fifteen thousand ...

ROBERTO *(indignant):* But why? Then I'll buy it myself ...

The Milanese immediately hands the watch to Roberto, with a very serious expression on his face.

MILANESE: You want to buy it? Then it's all yours, here ... *(To
   Augusto)* And as a matter of fact, if you do this kind of
   business, I, modestly speaking, can supply you with three
   dozen of these watches at one thousand five hundred apiece,
   carriage free ...

AUGUSTO *(grimly):* What do you mean, please?

MILANESE: I mean that I buy them at five hundred apiece at Lugano. And I also mean that my hair's turned white in this business. *(Raises his hat to reveal his white hair.)* Modestly speaking! *(To Roberto)* What will you have?

ROBERTO *(readily):* Likable chap, the old boy. A Campari!

Augusto takes back the watch and wraps it up again.

MILANESE *(to Augusto):* And you?

AUGUSTO: Well, I'll have a Negroni.

MILANESE *(to barman):* A Campari, a Negroni, and a lemonade. *(To Augusto)* I'm awfully sorry about it. *(He goes over to the cashier.)*

ROBERTO *(to Augusto):* But couldn't you tell he was a sharper?

Vargas enters with a large brief case under his arm; he is accompanied by Picasso.

VARGAS: Augusto!

ROBERTO: Here's the Baron.

Vargas gestures to them to join him in the adjoining room.

AUGUSTO *(to the barman):* Remember that the Milanese paid!

ROBERTO *(to the barman):* Bring the stuff in there, will you?

Augusto starts for the back room.

PICASSO: Hi, Augusto!

AUGUSTO: Hi.

PICASSO *(euphorically):* Well, it looks like everything's all set up for tomorrow morning. *(To Roberto, clapping a hand on his shoulder)* You know, Roberto, Vargas has had another terrific idea. On the outskirts of town ...

Picasso and Roberto follow Augusto into the back room.

Outskirts of Rome. Day.

The same black car drives down a lane on the far outskirts of Rome, followed by a mob of screaming children. The car pulls up in front of a group of shacks huddling around the ruins of an ancient aqueduct like an irregular, wretched bed of mushrooms. The children crowd around the car door shouting gaily.

The driver gets out and tries to shoo them away. It is Roberto, in the same chauffeur's uniform.

Inside sit Augusto and Picasso, all spruced up and carrying the same voluminous briefcase under his arm.

Picasso does not get out immediately; he seems somewhat wrought up and hesitates for a moment.

Augusto murmurs to him.

AUGUSTO *(curtly, softly):* Come on ... get a move on ...

Roberto opens the door.

ROBERTO *(to Picasso):* Here we are, Sir.

Picasso gets out and looks around. A whimpering child is sitting on top of one of the shacks; Picasso goes over to him and picks him up, smiling with simple spontaneous warmth.

PICASSO: Hey, what's wrong with you? Just look at him up there all by himself ... Who put you way up there? What are you doing? You're up in the mountains there. Don't cry. Come here, come here. Come here to me ... I'll take you down.

Roberto, leaning against the car, watches Picasso in amazement and turns to Augusto, still in the car.

ROBERTO: Augusto ... what's he up to?

PICASSO *(holding the child):* Ah, you don't want to tell me your name? Are you scared?

A short, swarthy man (Bevilacqua) comes out of the shack and comes aggressively up to Picasso to take back his child.

BEVILACQUA: Hey, what are you doing? Hey, this is my kid, you know!

PICASSO *(handing him the child):* I wasn't doing anything to him, you know, but he could have fallen off the roof ... *(Then, picking up his briefcase from the roof:)* In any case, could you please tell me ... could you tell me where ... hm ... where Mr. Sigismondo Giacotti lives?

He opens the brief case and consults some papers.

Bevilacqua turns and calls to a man leaning against one of the shacks.

BEVILACQUA: Hey, is Sigismondo Giacotti here?

MAN: He's gone to the hospital, hasn't he?

PICASSO *(hesitating for a moment):* Ah ... hm ... well, how about this other person ... Giovanni ... Bartoli?

BEVILACQUA: Giovanni Bartoli?

PICASSO: Yes.

BEVILACQUA *(pointing behind Picasso):* Try asking him.

An elderly man (Bartoli) comes up to Picasso with a suspicious expression.

BARTOLI: What do you want with Giovanni Bartoli?

PICASSO: Oh, no, nothing ... it was about the assignment of public housing apartments.

BARTOLI *(lighting up):* It's me!

BEVILACQUA *(quickly):* Oh, they're giving out the houses?

PICASSO: Of course!

BEVILACQUA: I applied two years ago.

BARTOLI: Me too, I applied two years ago ...

BEVILACQUA *(placing his finger on the papers):* Is Bevilacqua on the list? ... Bevilacqua ...

PICASSO: Bevilacqua?

Another man speaks up.

MAN: Hey, sir, I applied too, but nobody ever came around.

Picasso seems lost; he cannot answer everybody.

PICASSO *(hurriedly):* No, no, no, let's not confuse matters. The Commendatore's here ... he can explain everything. Come with me, come with me.

He starts back toward the car as the news of the assignment of the public housing spreads through the settlement.

Augusto watches Picasso from inside the car and puts on a pair of spectacles.

Other people pour out of the shanties and crowd noisily around the car as Picasso opens the door for Augusto. Roberto tries to keep back the crowd.

ROBERTO: Take it easy, take it easy ...

Augusto looks around with a good-natured, paternal smile.

An old man runs toward him and removes his hat.

OLD MAN: Hello, Commendatore. You people have finally woken up!

AUGUSTO *(somewhat severely to Picasso):* Did you explain everything clearly?

PICASSO: Yes, sir. I said we came about the houses. Ah, they tell me the first family lives over there.

AUGUSTO: Very good.

A woman calls to a distant friend.

WOMAN: They're giving us houses!

The friend answers with a sceptical smile.

FRIEND: Sure, houses!

Followed by Picasso and surrounded by the excited, shouting crowd, Augusto starts to walk through the two rows of shacks. Everyone is shouting confusedly, claiming rights of precedence in the assignment of the apartments.

A thin, dark-complexioned gypsy-looking fellow wearing a black cloak steps backward in front of Augusto, heatedly illustrating the injustice of his own situation.

MAN *(with Southern accent):* Commendatò, Commendatò, it's Providence that's sent you, Commendatò ... My name's Antonio. I applied for a house fourteen months ago ...

A woman in black comes out of a shack.

WOMAN *(screaming):* Who are they giving houses to anyway? To this good-for-nothing?

Augusto and Picasso continue to make their way through the shouting crowd.

CROWD: I asked two years ago. We applied four years ago, Commendatore. We've been waiting for two years. They're all a bunch of crooks.

Augusto and Picasso are almost knocked off their feet by the imploring crowd. Augusto stops.

AUGUSTO *(shouting impatiently):* Calm down, please, calm down. Will you please keep quiet?! *(The crowd quiets down)* The first apartments will be assigned this month.

BEVILACQUA *(carrying his child):* You people have been saying that for a long time, and we just don't believe you any more!

This stirs up the crowd, which begins to shout again.

Augusto lifts up his hands and invokes silence. He takes some papers from Picasso and waves them in the air.

AUGUSTO: Silence! One at a time. Here are the contracts ... They have to be signed and the first month's rent has to be paid down ...

The crowd's enthusiasm suddenly collapses. A frightened wave of embarrassment rapidly engulfs the little crowd of shanty dwellers, and the noise dies away.

A WOMAN: How much would it be?

AUGUSTO *(paternally severe):* It depends on the number of rooms ... It could be eight thousand, nine, nine thousand five hundred ... ten ... according to how many room ... It depends on the number of rooms, you see.

MAN *(coming forward):* What about those who can't pay?

AUGUSTO: Who can't pay the first month is still all right, he goes, onto the list for the next drawing and his apartment is assigned to the next person in line ... It's all in order ... according to when the requests were made ... The procedure is all very orderly, don't worry about that ...

Augusto waves the papers over his head.

Another moment of silence.

ANOTHER WOMAN: How much would it be for me? ... Ada Colangeli?

Augusto hands the papers back to Picasso, who has been admiring his unruffled performance.

AUGUSTO: Would you mind looking here for Ada Colangeli?

Picasso looks through the papers as the woman presses close to him, looking for her name. Others of the crowd ask about their own names.

OLD MAN: What about Luigi Fiorelli?

AUGUSTO: When did you apply?

OLD MAN: Three years ago.

AUGUSTO *(to an old woman):* And you?

OLD WOMAN: Mária Bove, Commendatore, Bo-ve!

AUGUSTO *(to another who carries a child):* And you?

WOMAN: Caterina Calabrò.

AUGUSTO: Calabrò? …

WOMAN: Caterina.

AUGUSTO: But you did make an application?

WOMAN: Yes, five months ago.

EMACIATED MAN *(standing in a doorway, protestingly):* I applied two
　　years ago!

The gypsy-like Antonio comes up aggressively behind Augusto.

ANTONIO: What d'you mean two years! You had a house and you
　　sold it! *(Then, to Augusto)* Commendatò, this guy doesn't
　　deserve any pity.

EMACIATED MAN *(venomously):* What do you mean? That wasn't my
　　house.

*A third man comes between the two; he is tall, wears a moustache
and is dressed with a propriety which sets him off from the others.*

TALL MAN: What d'you mean it wasn't yours? You were trying to sell
　　it to me!

A woman's voice invites Augusto into her shack.

VOICE OF WOMAN: Come in here, Commendatore.

Pressed by the crowd, Augusto and Picasso enter the shack as Roberto tries to hold the rest back from entering after them.

Inside shack. Day.

Augusto and Picasso follow the woman into the shack; she is falling all over herself in the effort to make them welcome. The shack contains a large bed, a table, a few ramshackle chairs, a dresser, and a cast-iron stove.

WOMAN: Please excuse me if it's sort of messy here. Please sit down, Commendatore, sit down … sit down.

Augusto sits down and places his papers on the table.

VOICE OF BEVILACQUA: What do you mean, I was the first one to talk to him, and now you won't even let me in?

ROBERTO: All right, one at a time.

AUGUSTO *(out of patience, trying to quiet the crowd):* Calm down! … Will you please calm down?!

Outside, still more shanty dwellers are running up to the shack.

Augusto takes out his pen and begins to check the names on the list. Then he notices a little boy who has suddenly appeared beside him. He caresses the child's head. Bevilacqua pushes his own boy toward Augusto.

BEVILACQUA: This is my little boy, Giorgio, say hello to the Commendatore.

Augusto pinches him affectionately on the cheek. Then a relative quiet follows.

AUGUSTO: Who's first?

PICASSO: Ernestina Giacotti.

VOICE *(through the crowd):* Here I am, Commendatore! God bless you!

PICASSO *(calling out another name from his list):* Gino Bevilacqua.

BEVILACQUA: Here I am! I'm right here.

PICASSO: Eight thousand five hundred lire.

AUGUSTO *(at the table, to Ernestina Giacotti):* Come here! Sign your name here.

PICASSO: Six thousand nine hundred lire ... Teresina Mingozzi.

A shaggy old man comes up behind Augusto, happily displaying his money.

OLD MAN: Commendatore, Commendatore! I've got money for it, you see? I've got nine thousand lire. My name is Giovanni De Felice.

A young woman makes her way through the throng with some effort waving some bills and calling to Augusto.

YOUNG WOMAN: Here you are! I have five thousand lire!

ANTONIO *(beside her):* Could you please lend me a thousand?

YOUNG WOMAN: Sure, I'm just about to lend money to you!

ROBERTO: Come on! Hurry up!

The shanty-dwellers continue to throng against the door of the shack, shouting and pleading.

Piazza Navona, Rome. Evening.

New Year's Eve: Piazza Navona is unusually animated. Stalls and booths of all sorts are lit up and decorated for the holiday. People walk along through the piazza laden with packages and bundles; firecrackers can be heard exploding.

Augusto and Picasso wander among the stalls, carrying packages in their arms.

Picasso is excited and gay as a child, while Augusto seems younger.

PICASSO: Oh, Augusto, listen, I have to give you ten thousand lire. *(He stops to look at the soap bubbles which an itinerant vendor is blowing nearby.)* Oh, I like that! Augusto, look. *(To the vendor)* Would you let me try, please?

VENDOR: Two hundred lire for the soap-bubble pipe! Lots of fun for the kids!

Picasso takes the little jar and the pipe and tries to blow bubbles, but is unsuccessful because he blows too hard.

PICASSO: Why doesn't it work?

VENDOR: Not that way, sir. You have to blow gently.

He shows Picasso how to blow. More bubbles come out of the pipe.

PICASSO: I get it; all right. Let me try. Blow gently. I get it! Augusto, watch this!

Picasso blows gently and this time succeeds.

Augusto watches Picasso, shaking his head in amusement.

VENDOR: See how much fun it is, sir? Buy it, it's only two hundred lire. You spend less and you make a child happy with only two hundred lire.

Picasso is enjoying himself like a child, and continues to blow soap bubbles.

PICASSO *(laughing):* It's cute, isn't it? Don't you like these things, Augusto? *(to the vendor)* Here, wrap it up for me.

AUGUSTO *(beginning to lose patience):* Let's go, let's go!

PICASSO: Yes, just a minute, I'll pay and we'll go. I want to bring it to Silvana. You know how she is. I'm sure she'll get a bigger kick out of this than anything else.

Picasso pays the vendor and starts off again with Augusto.

AUGUSTO: You're the one who's getting a kick out of it. You're just like a little kid.

(Car horn.)

An enormous, shiny Cadillac stops short just behind Augusto and Picasso. The two jump to one side, swearing.

AUGUSTO: What the hell?! ...

A loud, slow, jeering laugh emerges from the car, along with a string of insults directed at Augusto.

RINALDO: You bastard! ... Creep! ... Grave-digger! ... Two-timer! ... Turkey, ape, buzzard! What are you doing here?

Augusto, who has still not recovered from the shock, cannot make out who is at the wheel. The passenger is an extremely elegant young blond, covered with furs and jewels. Picasso stares wordlessly.

AUGUSTO *(venomously to the driver):* You sonuvabitch!

RINALDO *(laughing):* Augusto, it's me! Don't you recognize me? What are you up to?

Augusto suddenly recognizes the driver as a friend; his face lights up, with happy surprise.

AUGUSTO: Rinaldo!

Rinaldo leans over the wheel to smile at Augusto. He is a young enough man, but already bald, with great watery eyes and thick, sensuous lips.

RINALDO: Where are you going?

Caught off balance and already more servile, Augusto indicates Picasso.

AUGUSTO: I'm going to Piazza del Popolo ... but I have a friend here.

RINALDO: Oh, yes. Well, let him get in too and I'll take you there.

Without waiting for an answer, Rinaldo, still smiling, leans over the silent, haughty young woman and opens the door. He pushes her seat forward, forcing her to double over so that Augusto and Picasso can climb in. Augusto hurriedly tells Picasso to get in.

AUGUSTO *(softly):* Hop in, Picasso.

WOMAN *(protesting):* Oh, you're such a boor!

RINALDO: Keep quiet.

Augusto and Picasso scurry into the car like rats.

RINALDO: Just think, I run into you right on New Year's Eve.

PICASSO: Hello, Ma'am.

RINALDO: Hello, hello ...

The car reverses, then pulls out and they drive off.

In Rinaldo's car. Night.

Rinaldo is driving.

RINALDO *(still smiling):* Tell me, Augusto, who brought you the bread with the file inside this time?

AUGUSTO *(smiling at the joke):* The same baker that brought it to you.

Rinaldo laughs heartily.

The young woman passenger continues to maintain a tone of indifferent, discourteous haughtiness. She takes out a cigarette for herself; Rinaldo lights his own but not hers.

RINALDO: You know, it's been two years since we saw each other. What've you been up to all this time?

AUGUSTO *(admiring him and jealous):* The usual stuff. But what have you been doing? I see you're traveling like a prince. *(Rinaldo is very pleased.)* The last time I saw you, you were trying to con me out of five thousand lire ...

RINALDO: And I did con you out of five thousand! ... Augusto! Admit it!

AUGUSTO: No, you didn't con me out of anything at all.

RINALDO *(laughing):* What d'you mean? I did, I did, you can bet on that. *(Laughs.)* Now he says he don't remember because it makes him sick to think of it.

RINALDO *(turning to the young woman, Luciana):* You know who this character is? He's one of the ten plagues! He's conned half of Italy ... He's the big bad wolf! *(Laughs.)* Hell, he's worse than the wrath of God!

Luciana turns her head slightly, with a haughty nod for the introduction.

LUCIANA: Pleased to meet you.

RINALDO *(laughing):* You still going around with those skulls?

Augusto laughs somewhat crookedly and inclines his head slightly to acknowledge the introduction.

AUGUSTO *(jokingly to Luciana, indicating Rinaldo):* Do you know this gentleman very well, Ma'am?

Luciana does not respond to the joke; she continues to stare straight ahead.

RINALDO: Why don't you come to my place tonight? About ten. Listen, I want to see you, you know. I won't let you out of my sight this time.

Augusto is extremely flattered by the invitation, but somewhat perplexed.

AUGUSTO: Thanks, but ... I was going to be with this friend of mine...

RINALDO *(authoritarian):* All right, bring him, too. That's all right.

AUGUSTO: His wife was waiting for us, too, at home ...

RINALDO *(magnanimous):* Bring along your wife too! *(Rinaldo turns around a moment to look at Picasso and shake his hand.)* May I? Rinaldo Rossi. *(To Augusto)* Then I'll be waiting for you: Via Archimede 38, fourth floor. Don't come late or you'll miss the best of it.

Augusto and Picasso smile. Rinaldo stops the car and turns to Augusto.

RINALDO: Then I'll count on seeing you, eh? And look, if you don't show up I'll come dig you out, understand? *(To Luciana)* Let 'em out.

He opens Luciana's door and bends the seat forward as before, unconcerned about his companion's discomfort.

PICASSO *(getting out):* Sorry, Ma'am, sorry to disturb you ... there we are ... thanks ...

Augusto's heavy body gives him some trouble in getting out.

RINALDO *(jeering):* Eh, when are you going to get rid of that belly?! *(Laughs.)*

PICASSO *(bending to look in the window):* Thanks a lot. Goodbye, Ma'am; thanks.

AUGUSTO: So long. Goodbye, Ma'am.

The car departs as the two friends walk off.

PICASSO: Who was that?

AUGUSTO: You don't know who *that* was?!

Stairway to Rinaldo's house. Night.

Augusto, Picasso, and Iris come up the stairs dressed in their best clothes. Picasso is carrying a small painting under his arm.

A clamor of voices and music can be heard coming from the top floor. Augusto is clearly extremely excited and euphoric. Picasso and Iris are slightly apprehensive.

The noise of voices and music increases as they climb the stairs, with Augusto leading the way.

Augusto enters the apartment, where some couples are dancing, and greets someone. Iris becomes increasingly more nervous, and just before she and Picasso reach the top landing, she stops.

IRIS *(nervously):* I'm ashamed. I'm not coming.

Picasso, caught unaware, is puzzled.

PICASSO: What d'you mean ashamed?

Augusto, who has not heard, turns and beckons them on up.

AUGUSTO: Come on, come on in!

PICASSO: Come on, come on.

He takes Iris' arm and enters the apartment.

Rinaldo's apartment. Night.

Almost all the men are in tuxedos; the women's gowns tend to be very low cut. But the show of elegance each has sought to achieve by donning evening dress has largely evaporated by now. Young faces and old all express feline craftiness, toughness, aggressiveness, and vice; this is a gathering of very classy adventurers.

No one pays any attention to the newcomers. Augusto, Picasso, and Iris look around, feeling somewhat lost.

A haughty little waitress, who is trying to make her way through the crowd with a tray of half-filled glasses, passes between Augusto and Picasso.

WAITRESS: Let me through, please, let me through ...

Rinaldo comes toward her and, noticing the three new guests, exclaims hurriedly and festively.

RINALDO: Oh, here you are! ... Come on, come on ... Go over to the buffet and serve yourselves ...

PICASSO *(trying to introduce Iris):* My wife ...

But Rinaldo cannot even hear him through the uproar; he has already flung his arm around Augusto's shoulders and is leading him away, speaking softly, in an amused tone of voice.

RINALDO: Come here, come and look at this ...

He takes Augusto into the bedroom, which is as thronged as the other rooms.

A number of guests are surrounding a very young, well-built girl (Marisa), who is defending herself with an awkward and not terribly convincing attempt at modesty.

MARISA: But why? ... Can't you see like this?

A chorus of voices answers.

VOICES: No! ... Can't see a thing! ... What can we tell about what's underneath? ... With all the gadgets you have! ...

MARISA *(offended, spiritedly):* Sure! ... Gadgets! ...

Rinaldo intervenes with ostensible seriousness, pushing Augusto forward.

RINALDO: No, look, Miss ... just by coincidence this friend of mine's just come; he's a sculptor ... Let's agree to whatever he says.

Marisa looks at Augusto, half-convinced.

MARISA: You're a sculptor? ...

RINALDO: Of course he is ... He's even been to Terni. The monument to the con men ...

AUGUSTO: Of course.

An extremely excited little fellow pretends to speak very seriously.

GUEST: Excuse me, Miss. You want to enter the beauty contest? You want to have some probability of winning? That is, look, Miss, you say you have perfect breasts ... and we, forgive me, please ... we don't believe it ... so you'll have to demonstrate.

MARISA: But what do you want of me anyway?

RINALDO: You have to strip.

MARISA *(yields, exclaiming vexaciously):* Oh, all right!

She begins to strip.

GUEST: Thatagirl!

The atmosphere is boisterous and excited. A heavy man with a moustache pulls Iris off and begins dancing in a clownish way. Iris submits, intimidated and surprised.

Picasso sees Luciana and greets her by raising his glass, but she does not notice and continues on to the other room.

Rinaldo comes out and, instinctively on his guard, stretches his neck to see, without success.

LUCIANA: What are you up to? ... what's going on?

Rinaldo, annoyed, pushes her back.

RINALDO *(softly):* Nothing ... It's that dumb Marisa ...

LUCIANA: What's she doing?

RINALDO *(nastily):* Go on, get out of here! Go on, bitch.

He pushes her back. Luciana, vexed and glowering, goes back to join the crowd, pushing her way into the dining room.

Picasso and Iris, standing in one corner, are eating with hearty appetite. With his mouth full, Picasso makes Luciana a slight bow and tries to introduce Iris to her.

PICASSO: Iris, come here. I'd like to introduce my wife. Miss ... ah ... The lady is our hostess here.

IRIS: Pleased to meet you.

LUCIANA: Pleased to meet you.

Luciana goes off, throwing an uncomplimentary glance at Iris. Simultaneously, a young blond man sitting on the sofa behind which Picasso is standing turns his head. It is Roberto, who has heard Picasso's voice and greets him with amused, mocking amazement, laughing.

ROBERTO: Hey, Picasso. Who let you in?

PICASSO: Hello, Roberto. You're here too?

ROBERTO: Then this is really a low-class affair ... *(He greets Iris with neither enthusiasm nor cordiality)* Hello, Ma'am ...

PICASSO *(surprised but happy at this meeting):* We came with
Augusto …

*Roberto, who is reclining on the sofa next to a showy-looking elderly
woman with the depraved face of a dissolute old lady, pulls himself
up to a sitting position.*

ROBERTO: What? … Is the old man here, too?

PICASSO: We came with him.

*Roberto turns to his neighbor and addresses her politely in an
attempt at Spanish.*

ROBERTO: Excusame un momiento … *(Then he turns back to
Picasso with sudden interest)* Augusto knows the host
here?…

PICASSO: Yes … they're old friends … He gave us a lift today …
He's the one who invited us.

ROBERTO *(with growing interest, serious):* But … this guy is very big
… They tell me he made his pile with …

He puts a finger to his nose and sniffs, alluding to drugs.

PICASSO: Yes, I know.

ROBERTO: Oh, I didn't know. Where's Augusto.

*In the bedroom, the crowd presses tightly around Marisa, who is
now half-stripped. There is much excited laughter. Someone is
trying to finish undressing her, and the girl has pushed him away.*

MARISA: Give me my dress!

RINALDO: Let him, let him. I'm the one who said he could. *(Rinaldo
hands the girl a dressing gown)* That's enough now … she's
right … that's enough … Marisa, come get dressed … you'll
catch cold …

As the crowd laughs, Marisa wraps herself in the dressing gown and pushes away still another person.

MARISA: Get out of there! ...

Rinaldo pushes her toward the door of the other room.

RINALDO: Come here ... come in here ...

Augusto finds himself face-to-face with Roberto, and does not hide his annoyance, partially because he has been following Rinaldo. Roberto's tone of voice is still jeering, but he treats Augusto with new interest.

ROBERTO: Augusto! ... You look like a king tonight! ...

AUGUSTO *(dryly):* I know, I know ...

ROBERTO: The big boy's really your friend? ...

AUGUSTO: What do you want anyway? ...

ROBERTO: What are you two up to? ... Isn't there anything for me? I'm a friend ... You should remember at least that ...

Luciana makes her way through the throng and stops in front of the bathroom door, just a few feet away from Roberto and Augusto. She tries the door handle.

LUCIANA *(curtly):* Open up, Rinaldo!

GUEST: Look, there's no one in there, you know!

Luciana knocks repeatedly and angrily tries to force the handle.

LUCIANA: Open up, you bastard! ... Rinaldo if you don't open up right now there's going to be trouble.

Some people turn to observe the scene, Iris and Picasso among them.

Rinaldo's angry voice can be heard from the bathroom:

RINALDO: Cut it out, there's people here!

Luciana continues to beat on the door.

LUCIANA: I don't give a damn if there're people! ... Open up! ...

The door is suddenly opened and Rinaldo appears, enraged. Behind him the half-dressed girl, Marisa, can be seen. Rinaldo closes the door behind him.

RINALDO *(to Luciana):* I'll send you back to Mama, you know! This is some behavior. If that poor kid felt sick somebody had to help her, no? Come here. Gimme a little kiss.

LUCIANA *(with ostensible calm):* Sure, a little kiss. I'll give you a little kiss.

PICASSO *(smiling at Iris to minimize the episode):* They're kidding around.

Rinaldo takes Luciana's arm and leads her away from the door, talking in a hurried but reassuring tone.

RINALDO: Come on, come on. I'll get you something to drink. *(To the people crowding around them)* It's nothing, she got scared ... It's nothing.

He leads Luciana toward the buffet.

Picasso stops Rinaldo as he passes by and begins to unwrap the painting he has brought along.

PICASSO: Excuse me. I believe you're one of the few people who are capable of appreciating a really good painting, and so I've taken the liberty of bringing a little something along ...

Iris lights up with pride and hope.

Rinaldo does not even hear him, partly because Roberto, who has been awaiting his chance, steps in to introduce himself with his usual brazen assurance.

ROBERTO: May I? ... I'm a friend of Augusto's ... Roberto Giorgio ... I know this guy here too ... Congratulations, it's a terrific party ... really ... *(Rinaldo, who has immediately under-*

stood what sort of fellow this is, simply throws him some icy glances as he eats in silence.) Augusto's told me lots about you ...

Rinaldo does not even answer him; he turns to Picasso.

RINALDO: What were you saying?

PICASSO: Oh, no, I was saying that you seem to be a person that understands painting, and so I'd like ...

RINALDO *(interrupting him abruptly):* And you think I'm your man?

ROBERTO: You certainly know how a fine picture gives tone to a room. And a man of good taste like yourself ...

Picasso glances at Iris and Augusto; he has not the courage to pass the painting off as a real De Pisis. Rinaldo has understood.

RINALDO *(to Picasso):* Lemme see it.

PICASSO *(unwrapping the picture):* Yes, of course. This is a De Pisis.

RINALDO: You painted it? It's nice.

Picasso laughs, at once uncertain and astute.

PICASSO: No, what's that got to do with it, I have been painting for some years now, but ...

Rinaldo is no longer listening to him; he checks his watch and exclaims.

RINALDO: Hey, only ten minutes to go ... Turn on the TV ...

Picasso is mortified, but immediately recovers and turns to Iris with a smile.

PICASSO: I think he liked it.

Roberto approaches Augusto, who is serving himself at the buffet.

ROBERTO: Introduce me to this Rinaldo. I'm a very useful kind of boy.

AUGUSTO: What do you think, he needs guys like you? Don't make me laugh.

He goes off with the bottle in his hand. Roberto is offended.

ROBERTO: A fine friend you are ... I ask you ... Ah, you're going to pay for this, Augusto ... *(To the waiter)* Give me a whisky.

One of a small group of men sitting on the floor in a corner question Rinaldo.

FIRST CON MAN: Hey, Rinaldo, how much was it you got that time from that fire? ...

RINALDO *(chuckling, avoiding a direct answer):* I don't remember ... fifteen million ... sixteen ... I don't remember ...

The television set is transmitting sentimental music; a woman's voice sings "I Love You."

Augusto addresses Rinaldo with a smile and excessive nonchalance.

AUGUSTO: What? ... You don't remember? For Godsakes! ... You should have a secretary ... You know, I'd even do that for you ...

Rinaldo laughs and shouts to Luciana to call her attention to the music.

RINALDO: Luciana! ...

She comes over and Rinaldo starts dancing with her.

AUGUSTO *(insisting pathetically):* I'm really serious, you know?

RINALDO: You, with that face? ... My secretary? You'd get me arrested immediately.

He dances off, singing along with the music.

Augusto's smile freezes on his face; then he slowly follows Rinaldo.

TELEVISION VOICE: Only five minutes to go ...

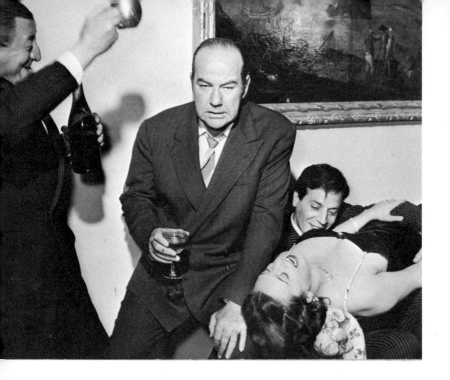

RINALDO *(shouting toward the kitchen):* Hey, the bottles ... Lina! ...
The champagne! ... *(He pushes Luciana rudely toward the
kitchen.)* She's just loafing ... You go see what's going on ...
The glasses, Lina ... The champagne! ... Lina! ... Were
you sound asleep? ...

*Luciana obeys as Lina, carrying a large tray, shouts from the kitchen
doorway.*

LINA: I had to wash them! ...

Rinaldo sits down beside Augusto, who leans over and talks to him.

AUGUSTO: I have to talk to you later. Let's have lunch together
tomorrow ... *(Rinaldo has taken out a cigarette.)* Wait, I'll
light it for you. *(He lights Rinaldo's cigarette.)* It's something
very important, you know? Listen.

RINALDO *(out of patience):* What is it? ... Tell me!

AUGUSTO *(with conviction, full of hope):* You remember the Texas
Club? I can get a three-year lease on it. In my own name, of
course. And I guarantee you thirty thousand a day ...

*Augusto is interrupted as the noise volume increases. Rinaldo is no
longer listening to him anyway. A short, swarthy man is dancing
with a handsome, well-built woman; they are the only ones dancing
and they are quite a comical picture. Rinaldo watches them, amused,
as Augusto tries to interest him in the proposition.*

AUGUSTO: Thirty thousand a night, doesn't that interest you?

RINALDO *(laughing, to the couple):* Pick 'im up! *(Rinaldo gets up, still smiling, and comes over to the little man. Augusto, disappointed, tries to hold him back.)* Pick 'im up, pick 'im up. It's midnight. Everything that's no good any more gets thrown out!

Rinaldo and some other men pick up the little man and start toward the window. The little man rebels, kicking and swearing, until they let him go.

LITTLE MAN: That's enough of these games! You're wrecking my new suit!

But three or four other guests catch him up again and carry him to the window, while another man sprays soda water in his face. Stripped of his trousers, the little man is suspended head down over the edge of the balcony, amid the explosions of firecrackers and pinwheels.

The noise of shouting, laughter, fireworks, and bottles crashing to the street increases in volume. Picasso and Iris toast each other and embrace affectionately.

IRIS: This year you'll have your show, eh?

PICASSO: Yes, yes.

Roberto, who has been keeping an eye on Augusto, finds himself surrounded for some moments by a group of wildly excited party-goers.

Lost in the noisy crowd, Augusto toasts the new year by himself, sadly.

Roberto's eyes fall on a gold cigarette case which a girl has left behind on an armchair. Roberto lets himself fall back into the armchair and slips the cigarette case into his pocket.

Now the glasses are brimming with champagne; all are wildly toasting the new year.

An hour later.

In the buffet room, the guests are dancing to the music from the radio.

Among the couples are Iris and Picasso, who dance tightly together, almost immobilized in the general confusion. Picasso speaks into Iris' ear with serious conviction.

PICASSO: You know what we'll do one of these days? We'll go to Venice ... Because you absolutely have to see Venice ... You can't imagine ... and then, just think how much fun Silvana would have in a gondola ... *(Suddenly)* Or should we go to Taormina? Think how great it would be in the winter now.

IRIS: No, Venice would be better ... It's more poetic. *(Pause)* But I'd need an evening gown ...

PICASSO: Of course you would! We'll get one ...

IRIS: Carlo ... I look awful this way, don't I ...

PICASSO: No, why?

IRIS: They all have these beautiful evening gowns on, and I'm like this ... If I'd known I wouldn't have come.

PICASSO: Of course not, you're still the prettiest of them all. If you weren't already my wife I'd be after you tonight, you know?

Laughing, they embrace.

IRIS: Oh ... my head's dizzy. Maybe I've drunk too much. But the champagne's good, isn't it?

PICASSO: It sure is.

A girl sitting on the couch looks around as if searching for something.

GIRL: Excuse me, you didn't happen to see a gold cigarette case?

VOICE OF WOMAN: No, I'm sorry.

Roberto strolls among the couples with a glass in his hand and sits down on the couch. Luciana, standing by the door, is staring at him with somewhat strained attention. Roberto's eyes meet hers; he masks his uneasiness with a smile and raises his glass to toast her. Luciana stares at him.

The old Spanish woman approaches Roberto and says something affectionate to him in her language. Roberto, who does not understand, answers.

ROBERTO: What are you saying?

SPANISH WOMAN: It is midnight. You not give me even little kiss. *(Roberto grimaces in annoyance.)* Kiss me.

Roberto kisses her cynically but she pulls him tightly to her and bites his ear. Roberto reacts crudely.

ROBERTO: Hey, don't you act like a slut with me, you'll get me filthy. Stupid! *(Turning to Iris and Picasso, who are passing nearby and have stopped to watch)* You people going to stay much longer?

PICASSO: Yes, sure.

ROBERTO *(glancing at the old lady):* See this chick here, she's got five million on her head alone.

PICASSO: Who is she?

ROBERTO: Some old lady. I don't know ... *(He turns to her and says affectionately, giving her a pinch on the cheek:)* Ugly!

The old lady smiles. Picasso and Iris start dancing again, amused.

Augusto has managed to catch Rinaldo again in the bedroom, where the host is stretched out on the bed with Marisa and gives some sign of being drunk.

Sitting on the floor near the bed, Augusto talks to Rinaldo as the latter listens distractedly while caressing Marisa.

AUGUSTO: We open a loan office in some small town. Even if it should go bad, I'm the one who will have to pay, because it'll be in my name, no?

Rinaldo continues to caress Marisa's head. Augusto touches his arm.

AUGUSTO: Hey, Rinaldo, you'll put it in my name, won't you?

RINALDO *(cold and distant, turning to stare at him):* Put what?

AUGUSTO: What d'you mean, what? The loan office, no?

RINALDO *(laughs):* Haven't you got it through your head yet that I don't give a damn about these things any more? *(Staring at Augusto)* Say, tell me something. How old are you?

AUGUSTO *(bewildered, smiling crookedly):* Why?

RINALDO: Tell me how old you are. I want to know.

AUGUSTO: Forty-eight ...

RINALDO *(laughing cruelly):* And at your age you're still thinking about fooling around? You really surprise me, you know? It's disgraceful.

Augusto's smile freezes on his lips; he is crushed by Rinaldo's indifference and irony.

Luciana appears in the doorway.

LUCIANA: Rinaldo!

Vexed, Rinaldo turns slightly toward her.

RINALDO: What is it? ...

LUCIANA *(urgently):* Come here a minute ...

RINALDO: What do you want anyway? ...

LUCIANA: Come here a minute.

RINALDO *(getting up with effort, slowly, obviously irritated):* What a pain.

Luciana says something softly and seriously to Rinaldo, who smiles briefly. He starts toward the front door, almost staggering.

At the door, Iris, Picasso, and Roberto are preparing to leave. Roberto winds a silk scarf around his neck; as he sees Rinaldo, he addresses him with his usual bantering voice and brazen assurance.

ROBERTO: Oh, here's our hospitable host! ... I was looking for you to thank you for this magnificent evening, and to wish you the very best for the coming year.

IRIS: Thank you.

PICASSO: We really thank you.

RINALDO *(staring into Roberto's eyes):* Listen ... There's a girl in there that's lost her cigarette case ...

ROBERTO *(displaying regret):* Really? The poor girl ... I'm sorry ... Of course it's what you'd expect, with all this confusion.

RINALDO: The cigarette case happens to be gold.

ROBERTO: Sorry, I don't understand.

Picasso and Iris hold their breath. Iris still does not fully understand. Picasso looks at Roberto in alarm. Augusto appears just behind Rinaldo, and other people are gathering about. Roberto's bearing is still self-assured.

RINALDO: You don't understand! You didn't happen to find it, did you? You know, lots of times a person might be thinking of something else and doesn't remember. And then, when they get home, they find it.

He laughs as he stares at Roberto.

ROBERTO: You know, I still don't understand.

Rinaldo laughs again. Another man whispers to him.

MAN: You know this guy's really a scream?

RINALDO: You know what I'd do if I were you?

ROBERTO: No, what?

RINALDO: I'd start looking for it and I'd find it.

LADY *(to the swarthy little man):* What's going on?

LITTLE MAN: I have the impression, dear Countess, that somebody's pinched something.

ROBERTO: Listen, the thing is ... Of course I'd be very glad to do it, but you know, I ... *(Augusto is staring severely at Roberto. Roberto glances at him and then feigns aggressive astonishment)* What is this anyway? ... What do you want from me? ... Excuse me, what kind of a way to talk is that?

RINALDO *(calm, sure of himself):* My friend, you got a long way to go ... before you can come play around in here ... The lady wants to smoke — offer her a cigarette, no?

ROBERTO *(trying to react once more):* You mind telling me what you're driving at?

RINALDO *(with icy calm):* Come on, make believe you were just joking, no? You say you were joking and everybody'll be happy. *(Shouting angrily)* Well, you going to tell us you were joking, yes or no?

Roberto looks around. There is an icy pause; then, with a slight smile, he goes over to the woman Rinaldo has indicated, takes the gold cigarette case out of his pocket, opens it and holds it out to her.

ROBERTO: Well, yes, I was joking. *(To the lady)* You got scared, didn't you? I was just joking.

The lady takes the cigarette case; Rinaldo throws an ironic kiss to Roberto and opens the door.

LADY: Thanks.

ROBERTO: You're welcome. *(To Rinaldo)* Satisfied?

RINALDO: My God!

Only slightly embarrassed, Roberto waves broadly to the crowd.

ROBERTO: Happy New Year to everybody!

He departs.

RINALDO *(turning to Augusto):* Augusto, what the hell kind of friends do you have anyway?! And you go around with them too?

Augusto is standing stock-still.

Iris is pale as death.

Picasso is mortified.

They hurry out.

Rinaldo begins to dance with Luciana.

RINALDO: Hey, Lucy, sew up your pockets!

Via Archimede. Night.

Roberto, Picasso, Iris, and Augusto come out of the doorway to Rinaldo's building into the deserted street.

Iris is still tense and horrified. Picasso, profoundly disturbed, calls to her from behind.

PICASSO: Iris!

Iris does not answer. She is about to cry. Roberto, exaggerates his nonchalance.

ROBERTO *(loudly):* Which way are you people heading?

Picasso does not answer.

AUGUSTO *(dryly):* You're supposed to be a sharp guy, eh?

Iris runs across the street.

PICASSO *(calling):* Iris!

Roberto assumes an attitude of bored superiority; he looks around.

ROBERTO: It's no joke to find a taxi at this hour!

Augusto comes up face-to-face with Roberto, but restrains himself from hitting him.

AUGUSTO: If your mother wasn't worse than you she'd have strangled you when you were born.

ROBERTO *(detached, indifferent):* Yes, I know ... You're right, but don't spit in my face ...

Enraged, Augusto grabs Roberto's lapel.

Picasso has stopped not far off and is uncertain whether to follow the fleeing Iris or to stop the imminent fight.

PICASSO: What are you two up to? Augusto ...

Provocatively calm and sardonic, Roberto removes Augusto's hand:

ROBERTO: Augusto. At your age you shouldn't ... *(Then he shouts to a passing taxi:)* Taxi! *(The cab stops; he shouts to Augusto:)* So long, go to bed, go on! *(He climbs in and the taxi pulls off:)* Happy New Year!

Augusto, very tense, remains standing there. Picasso, who sees Iris continuing to walk on, would prefer to put off the encounter with her.

PICASSO: Augusto ... Come on along with us. Come with us.

Augusto starts down the deserted street, on the far side from Iris.

AUGUSTO: No, good night.

After a last moment's hesitation, Picasso runs after Iris.

PICASSO *(calling):* Iris! Iris!

Iris' face is strained. Picasso makes an effort to keep his tone natural.

PICASSO: What kind of a thing was that to do? A gold cigarette case.

He must have been drunk. He was certainly drunk.

Iris does not answer. Picasso takes out his cigarettes.

PICASSO *(solicitously):* Want a smoke?

IRIS *(her voice distorted, abruptly):* What are you doing with those people? Why do you go around with them? ... What do you all do together? ...

PICASSO *(disturbed and uneasy):* Nothing ... We work ...

IRIS: What is it you do with Roberto, and that other man? ... What kind of work is it? ...

PICASSO: But you know ... What are you thinking now? I've always told you everything ...

She does not answer; she barely manages to fight back her tears, and her eyes express bewildered terror.

IRIS: I never know anything! You never tell me the truth ...

Silence. Picasso is disturbed; he seems about to make a confession, but he saves himself.

PICASSO: I'm not like them ... What do you think, I want to ruin myself? I ... I work ... I don't do anything wrong ... *(Pause; then, more bitterly)* I've got to do something to support you ...

Iris finally breaks out in a desperate, almost hysterical sob.

IRIS: But what have you got to do? ... Steal? ... You have to end up in jail?

PICASSO *(truly frightened):* Iris, please ... Darling, it's New Year's.

Iris weeps.

PICASSO: Let's not begin the year this way. Be good.

IRIS *(sobbing):* I knew very well what kind of people they were. And how many times did I tell you ... and you nothing, ever ...

always lies ... You come, you go, I don't know where your money comes from, you're in trouble all over the place, and every time somebody knocks on the door my heart skips a beat. I can't take it any more.

Iris has stopped. Picasso comes up to her, and the two walk along together in silence.

PICASSO *(moved and worried, softly):* Iris! Don't be like that. Don't act like that. I beg of you, calm down. I, I love you, Iris. I'll do whatever you want. I swear it. Look, I won't go with those guys any more. They'll never see me again, never again. I'll find a way to earn something. I'll sell my pictures.

IRIS *(drying her tears):* Oh, I can't believe you any more.

PICASSO: You're right, I know. But I ... I swear I'll change my ways. I swear it to you, Iris. Believe me, my love.

IRIS: You always talk like that.

PICASSO: Yes, it's true. But you know that I have only you and the baby. I think only of you two. *(Weeps.)*

IRIS: You know I don't care anything about money. I'm not afraid. It's enough for me that you go back to the way you used to be, when were were just married. *(Picasso takes her hand and kisses it affectionately.)* Oh, sure, now you kiss my hand.

She turns, embarrassed and pleased.

PICASSO: You want to smoke now?

IRIS: Yes. *(Picasso laughs, touched and happy.)* You'll see what I'll do to you one of these days. Sure, go on and laugh.

They light their cigarettes, again at peace with each other.

PICASSO: Well then, Happy New Year! *(They hear festive noises down the street.)* Hey, sweetheart, shall we go see what's going on down there? Come on, let's go!

He takes her arm and they go off quickly.

A piazza. Day.

A few hours later. It is a dreary New Year's Day morning; the piazza is deserted, with no sign of life.

The pavement is strewn with fragments of broken pots, paper streamers and pieces of newspaper, which the wind whips around.

Augusto walks along all alone, now and then kicking a tin can. He feels exhausted, and above all fears going home to be alone with himself and his defeat.

Two prostitutes accost him.

PROSTITUTE: Hey, Happy New Year! Where you going? Stop a minute. Come with us! Any better way to start the new year?

SECOND PROSTITUTE: We'll bring you good luck. Come here. Too bad!

Augusto continues on his way without answering.

Piazza di Spagna. Day.

A month later, early on a radiant spring morning. The flower vendors are opening their baskets at the bottom of the Spanish Steps.

Augusto is waiting on the steps; his expression is happy, unconstrained, almost youthful.

A very showy custom-built sports car turns into the piazza and stops not far from him, honking its horn briefly. Roberto is at the wheel.

ROBERTO *(shouting):* Hey, dad! Augusto? Augusto! Here I am. Come on! *(Augusto comes up to the car, observing it in some surprise.)* Classy, eh?

AUGUSTO: Whose car is this anyway?

ROBERTO: Come on, get in, get in!

Augusto opens the door and climbs in. The car pulls off immediately.

ROBERTO: You'd like to know, wouldn't you? *(Singing)* But my mystery is locked in my heart.

Piazza del Popolo. Day.

Picasso is waiting at the entrance to the café, with a brief case under his arm. He sees the car.

PICASSO: Hey!

ROBERTO *(pointing):* There he is. *(Leans out of the car and calls)* Picasso!

Picasso starts forward, but the car, which had slowed down, now suddenly guns ahead.

Roberto and Augusto laugh at the trick. The car stops a few yards further on. Picasso catches up, laughing and panting from his sprint.

PICASSO *(pleased):* Hey, what a great car! We going in this? Where are the coats? Let me try one on a minute.

Augusto takes an overcoat from a stack of about twenty coats that are carefully folded up on the back seat.

ROBERTO: Sure, but take it easy when you put it on. They cost sixteen hundred apiece.

Picasso puts on the coat.

ROBERTO: Hey, they're really not bad at all.

PICASSO: Sure, but look, sixteen hundred's sixteen hundred. That's really a swindle, you know?

ROBERTO *(somewhat irritated):* Next time you go buy them, you're an artist and you'll get them for less ... What d'you mean, just the new buttons Mama put on cost what they cost. *(Cautions him comically.)* Take it easy, be careful, don't bend your arm or the whole sleeve'll come out ... Don't put your hands in your pockets! Don't wake up the moths!

PICASSO *(giving him something from the pocket to smell):* Smell this!

ROBERTO: Um, smells of mice. Come on, get in.

Picasso gets in the car.

ROBERTO *(to Augusto):* Augusto, please go buy some cigarettes.

PICASSO: Say, how much are we paying to rent this car?

ROBERTO: Zero point zero. It's the old bitch's. She's stoned. And she won't wake up for three days. *(To Augusto)* Augusto, get a move on, get the cigarettes!

Augusto goes toward the café, and encounters a group of students walking toward the Pincio.

The students are talking and laughing among themselves, almost blocking the sidewalk. Augusto has already passed by them when one of the girl students stops and stares at him.

PATRIZIA: Papa!

Augusto stops short and does an about-face. He looks at the girl; his expression suddenly changes.

AUGUSTO: Patrizia!

PATRIZIA *(moving a few steps toward him):* Papa!

AUGUSTO *(looking at the girl with a half smile of embarrassment and surprise):* Oh, how you've changed! ... I wouldn't have recognized you ... really.

Patrizia half smiles in embarrassment too. Now one of her companions notices that she has stopped, and turns to call her.

GIRL STUDENT: Patrizia! Patrizia, what are you up to there?

PATRIZIA *(gesturing to her friend to wait):* I'll be right there.

AUGUSTO: No school today?

PATRIZIA: No, it's math so we all left early.

AUGUSTO: Out for a walk, eh?

PATRIZIA: Yes!

She does not continue. Augusto changes the subject.

AUGUSTO: How's Mama?

PATRIZIA: She's all right ... She had a little flu but now she's better. *(Smiles.)*

PATRIZIA *(calling to her friends once again):* Just a minute, I'll be right there!

AUGUSTO: Go on, go on ... They're waiting for you ... You know, one of these days I'll come see you ... or ... I'll call you.

PATRIZIA *(somewhat incredulous):* Fine.

AUGUSTO: Really, I will. I promise you.

PATRIZIA: Yes, yes.

AUGUSTO: So long, Patrizia.

PATRIZIA: So long, Papa.

He comes closer, takes her hands and kisses her with a familiarity that is unnatural to him.

Almost pulling away from Augusto's hand, Patrizia returns to her companions without looking back.

Augusto stands there some moments gazing at the curly head disappearing in the crowd, and waves uncertainly.

Inside the car. Day.

Roberto, Augusto, and Picasso drive along the Via Flaminia about forty kilometers outside Rome. Augusto is silent. A gas station comes in sight around a curve.

Country gas station. Day.

The car slows down and stops beside the pumps. Roberto gets out as the attendant, an elderly, bald, neat man in overalls comes quickly over to the car. In his usual bantering, brazenly impudent manner, Roberto greets him in English.

ROBERTO: Hello, boy! ... *(Handing him the trunk key)* Ten liters.

The man is a little slow but extremely meticulous as he turns the pump handle to zero the gauge.

ATTENDANT: Extra? ...

ROBERTO: Superextra!

The attendant opens the trunk and rests the gas hose in the gas tank.

ROBERTO *(inhaling deeply):* You live well out here, eh? Nothing to do from morning to night ... And you make a pile of money. Isn't that right?

ATTENDANT *(smiling resignedly, playing along with the joke):* You've hit it right on the nail. All the land here belongs to me, too! *(Then, after a sigh)* Ah, if you only knew, dear sir ...

Roberto gazes at him in silence.

ROBERTO *(then, with exaggerated indignation):* God Almighty! The truth is that a man works his whole life long, and afterwards he ought to have the right to rest! What kind of hours do you keep?

ATTENDANT: There are no hours. If you want to eat every day ... you have to stay here at night too.

ROBERTO: Even at night?

The attendant hangs the gas hose back on the pump and closes the tank.

ATTENDANT: Oil? Water? ...

ROBERTO: No, take a look at the tires. See how they are.

ATTENDANT: Right away.

As the old man hurries to do so, Roberto winks at Augusto and Picasso, who are following his operations from inside the car.

ROBERTO: How much is it?

ATTENDANT: Thirteen hundred and eighty lire.

ROBERTO: Fine. *(Then, with extreme self-assurance)* Oh, but look, I'm not paying you, you know. *(The attendant smiles in amusement.)* Because it so happens, old boy, that I'm broke and I have to be in Terni at the Prefecture at twelve-thirty.

Here's what we'll do, look ...

Roberto interrupts himself, pretending to think. The old attendant, disconcerted, has stopped filling the tires and watches Roberto, waiting for him to go on. Roberto continues as if he has finally figured out a solution.

ROBERTO: You give me ten thousand lire; ten plus thirteen hundred eighty for the gas is eleven thousand three hundred and eighty. This evening, when I go back to Rome, I'll give you thirteen thousand ... All right? ... You understand? ... Answer.

The old man has not understood well; he is extremely uncertain.

ATTENDANT: But ... what do you mean?

ROBERTO *(leaning toward him):* What? ... What did you say?

ATTENDANT: I just said what do you mean.

ROBERTO *(smiling):* You don't trust me? ... Come on, you don't trust me? ...

ATTENDANT: No, I trust you, but I don't understand.

ROBERTO *(resigned and understanding):* All right ... Take my coat ... *(He turns to the other two with an air of amused superiority.)* Understand? Give me my coat ... *(Laughs.)*

Picasso plays his part readily as Augusto, serious, looks from one to the other.

ATTENDANT: It's not that I don't trust you, you know, but I'm responsible ...

ROBERTO: Let's give him my coat. Look, is that enough for security?

ATTENDANT: Yes.

PICASSO *(indignant and surprised):* What are you doing? ... You're giving him a fifty-thousand lire coat for ten thousand? ...

Roberto shrugs his shoulders and holds the coat out to the old man, without handing it over, however.

ROBERTO: What else can I do? Poor old guy, he doesn't trust me. *(To the old man, jokingly)* You wouldn't mind if I didn't come back to pick it up, would you?! ... Don't touch it, your hands are filthy with oil. *(Before handing him the coat, Roberto pretends to search the pockets.)* Oh, wait a minute ... This would be a little too much. *(He pulls a watch out of the coat pocket and puts it in his trousers pocket.)* The watch was still in there. That would've been a real bargain, eh?

ATTENDANT: I trust you because you're a gentleman.

ROBERTO *(taking his arm and leads him to the office):* Some trust; I'm leaving you this. Show me where you're going to put it.

ATTENDANT: Come on over here.

ROBERTO *(to Augusto and Picasso):* He's a real friend, the old guy.

Inside the car. Day.

Roberto whistles as he drives; Picasso tries to hum along with him. Augusto looks straight ahead in silence.

Another gas station appears through the windshield.

The car slows down ...

Second gas station. Day.

... and stops in front of the gas pumps. A boy of about fifteen, dressed in overalls, comes out of the office; his face is childish, smiling and solicitous. He greets them cheerfully.

ATTENDANT: Hello! ...

AUGUSTO: Hello.

ATTENDANT: Gas?

AUGUSTO: Ten liters of extra.

ATTENDANT: Is the gas tank in back?

AUGUSTO: Yes.

Augusto gets out as the boy hurries to set the gauge, open the trunk and pump in the gas.

Augusto stands by the pump. Picasso hands him a coat, which Augusto folds carefully to hide the defects.

Piazza of country town. Day.

The central piazza of a Latian town has been taken over by a traveling amusement park. The screechy music of a carousel merges with the pitch coming over a loudspeaker.

Augusto, Roberto, and Picasso are coming down a flight of stairs.

Roberto and Picasso, a little high, are gaily joking and singing together. Augusto remains somewhat detached and silent.

Picasso is carrying a flask of wine; he climbs up onto the railing of the stairway and begins to walk the tightrope.

PICASSO: Olè, olè! ... Attention, Messieurs. S'il vous plaît, attention...

At a certain point he pretends to slip. Roberto catches his hand and steadies him.

ROBERTO *(continuing down the steps, pointing):* Oh look, there's the muscle-gauge.

PICASSO: Oh, great!

VOICE: Test your muscles!

They are now in one section of the amusement park.

ROBERTO *(to Picasso):* Well, should we try it?

PICASSO: Let's go, of course. *(Augusto has stopped behind them. Picasso calls to him)* Augusto, you remember this song?

VOICE: Test your muscles!

Dancing along to the rhythm of the music, Picasso and Roberto go off happily toward the stalls.

Country town. Night.

The town clock rings ten times.

Augusto, Roberto, and Picasso come out of the local hotel-restaurant at the end of a narrow street. Augusto and Roberto, absorbed in their own thoughts, walk along with their hands in their pockets.

Roberto sings softly as he looks around; Augusto is silent and rather grim.

Picasso remains somewhat apart from them. His coat is wide open; he is obviously drunk, and stumbles along by himself.

PICASSO: Hey, let's go see the medieval castle!

AUGUSTO: Forget it, stupid!

ROBERTO: What a pain that dumbbell is! *(Roberto comes over to a door and cocks his ear to listen.)* Quiet, quiet ... Oh, it's a stable. *(He starts off with Augusto again.)* Can it be that there's not a single woman in this whole town? Not a one, eh? *(He looks down a side street, shouting.)* Hey, women! Can you imagine what kind of people live here? It's enough to make you commit suicide.

Behind them, Picasso has taken off his coat and waves it around in the air as he reels along.

PICASSO: Ladies and gentlemen! Pure English wool! Guaranteed craftsmanship! Pure wool! ...

He holds the coat up to the wind, jabs two fingers through the fabric as if it were paper, and pulls it over his head, continuing to shout drunkenly:

PICASSO: Very durable! ... Crease-resistent! ... Hey, look out for the corrida! Ready to run the bull through! ... Olè!!

He starts to run toward Roberto and Augusto, imitating a bull.

AUGUSTO: Look out or you'll break your head open! Here he comes, let's go.

They walk on. Picasso has come to a stop with his shoulders against a wall; he laughs unemotionally.

Suddenly he turns serious and stares at an image of the Holy Virgin set into the wall of one of the houses.

He approaches the little altar and stares at it as if seized by remorse. Then he goes to hide behind the corner of a wall, peeping out once again to look at the effigy.

Augusto and Roberto continue walking along slowly. Roberto whistles.

AUGUSTO *(suddenly, in a dull voice):* We have to think about doing something more serious. We certainly can't go on this way.

Roberto's answer is marked with aggressive and ironic thought-lessness and levity.

ROBERTO: Who wants to go on this way? I'm not as stupid as you think. These are little games, to have some fun. *(They stop in front of a little door)* But I sing ... As soon as I have a little money I'm going to study seriously ... *(Volubly, without transition)* I've already bought all of Johnny Ray's records. Every last one. That's just the style for me.

Augusto shrugs his shoulders.

AUGUSTO *(softly and dryly):* You'll never study ...

Roberto is not hurt by this comment.

ROBERTO *(with ironic cruelty):* You don't think I want to end up like you, do you? ... *(Declaiming)* I have your example before me, dear old man! I have your example ... *(Sings.)* dear old man ... I have your example! ...`

Their attention is caught by the voice of Picasso, who is kicking at the wind in the center of a piazza containing a number of amusement-park rides.

PICASSO *(shouting):* Augusto!

ROBERTO *(to Augusto):* What an animal! Let's go see. *(To Picasso)* Picasso, cut that out!

Picasso jumps onto the platform of the "Flying Seat," clutches one of the seats and shakes it.

PICASSO: Come on, I'll treat everybody. How much you think it is?

Augusto, who has come up with Roberto, seizes Picasso in a rage and shakes him.

AUGUSTO: Come on, let's go.

PICASSO *(trying to get loose):* No, no. I want to take a ride ... Lemme go, where are you taking me?

Augusto catches him again and pushes him away. Roberto observes the scene from nearby.

AUGUSTO: Will you quit it?! Look here. Look what kind of shape you're in!

Picasso sways and reels even more markedly.

PICASSO: Augusto, how much you think one of these contraptions costs? Roberto, one of these ride things, how much ...

Picasso staggers a few steps forward, then falls to his knees, rolling his eyes and whimpering.

AUGUSTO: You see that? You see what happens when you make him drink?

PICASSO: I feel sick ...

ROBERTO: What, I made him drink? Two glasses. He's just a weakling.

AUGUSTO *(bending over Picasso to help him to his feet):* Sure, two glasses! You made him drink two liters!

ROBERTO: Leave him alone, leave him!

PICASSO *(whimpering):* Lemme stay here.

AUGUSTO *(to Roberto):* You know perfectly well he just has to smell wine to get stoned.

ROBERTO *(protesting):* What d'you want?

AUGUSTO: He's enjoying himself now, he's really having fun.

Meanwhile he has gotten Picasso up and half carries him over to a fountain.

AUGUSTO: Come on, come here and wash your face! *(Picasso reaches the fountain with Augusto's help, then doubles over.)* Come on!

Augusto pushes Picasso's head under the stream of water. Picasso resists but Augusto holds him firmly.

ROBERTO: Come on, get him in the neck!

Picasso continues to yelp, trying to get away.

PICASSO: Ow, ow, it's burning! *(He manages to make his escape and rushes Augusto, hitting his arm.)* Leave me alone!

AUGUSTO: Ow! ...

Wiping his neck on his coat, Picasso goes off, still whimpering, and sits down on the railing of a stairway.

PICASSO: You guys leave me alone!

Roberto calls someone who is passing through the far end of the piazza.

ROBERTO: Hey, hey you!

He begins to run in that direction; Augusto turns to shout after him:

AUGUSTO: Where are you going now?

ROBERTO: I'm going to ask this guy something.

AUGUSTO: Wait for us, will you?!

He approaches Picasso again.

PICASSO: Leave me alone ... Go away ... you too, Augusto .. Get out of here!

AUGUSTO *(sitting down in front of him):* How do you feel?

Picasso breathes heavily; intoxication has plunged him into a state of dejection.

PICASSO *(murmuring):* I feel bad, that's how. *(He staggers to his feet as if he has made some sudden, drunken decision, and starts down the stairs.)* Do whatever you want to ... I'm going home. You go right on to Florence if you want to. Don't worry about me ... I want to go home because I feel bad.

AUGUSTO *(rising and following him):* Where do you think you're going? Can't you see you can't even stand up? *(Picasso stops and leans against the wall. Augusto takes Picasso's coat off.)* Come on, come here, take this thing off ... and walk a little, it'll do you good.

He tries to drag him along, but Picasso collapses on the steps.

Picasso starts to weep, squeezing his cheeks between his palms;

finally he talks brokenly.

PICASSO: Some day I'm going to go home and I won't find her there
... I shouldn't have come this morning ... Iris asked me so
many questions ... She's suspicious. One of these days she'll
leave. I musn't come with you anymore. Iris suspects
something, I'm sick of lying to her ... She might just do it,
one day she'll take the baby and go to her mother's ... But if
she takes the baby away I'll kill myself ...

He lies down on the steps, his head cradled in one arm.

*Augusto gazes at him with a mixture of compassion and stony scorn,
but in reality he is disturbed.*

AUGUSTO: What got into your head anyway, to get married at
eighteen? ... You ruined yourself ... What can you do now?
You're ruined, ruined ... *(He stops as if to get hold of
himself, then says more curtly.)* You better find some other
profession ... You're not cut out for this kind of work ...
Change your work, look for something better.

*Picasso raises his head and looks at Augusto somewhat bewildered,
almost mortified.*

PICASSO: Why? ... I've got the right kind of face ... You always told
me yourself, that with my face ... I can con whoever I want
... I look like an angel. You can leave me anywhere in the
world, even where I don't know anybody, and I'll always
manage.

AUGUSTO *(gazing at him with scorn and pity):* Say a million ...

PICASSO *(not understanding):* Why? ...

AUGUSTO: Come on, come on, you understand. Say a million ...

*Picasso still hesitates; then, uncertainly, bleakly, his face pouring
water, he murmurs.*

PICASSO: A million ... *(Laughs.)*

AUGUSTO: You see you can't even say it, and you know why, because you can't even imagine a million. As soon as you have four bits you run to take them to your wife, poor fool! ...

PICASSO: Augusto, I ...

Augusto continues to speak softly, but increasingly excited.

AUGUSTO: In our kind of work you can't have a family. A man's got to be free to come and go, to get up and leave whenever he wants to. You can't be tied to your wife's apron strings. You have to be a loner. When you're young, the most important thing is to be free, even more important than the air you breathe. If you're scared now, think of when you'll be as old as me. The years go by, you know? *(He stops suddenly. After a moment he pulls Picasso to his feet.)* Come on, get up now. Come on, up. *(Picasso rises slowly, with effort, and starts down the stairs again with Augusto.)* It'll do you good to get some air.

Picasso mumbles something unintelligible.

AUGUSTO: You feel better now!

PICASSO: Yes, I feel better. But I'm not coming to Florence. I'm going home ...

AUGUSTO: Oh come on! ... We'll have some fun in Florence ... we've got a lot of dough ...

PICASSO *(softly, obstinately):* No, no, I'm going home ...*(Stops and suddenly says to Augusto:)* But Augusto ... how do you do it? ... I admire you, I wish I had your courage. How can you keep it up at your age? ... Don't you ever get scared?

AUGUSTO *(profoundly bewildered for a moment):* Scared of what?

PICASSO *(dejected):* No, I'm not like you, no ... I *(He looks up at the black sky.)* It's beginning to rain.

Roberto appears at the top of the stairs, in the company of a brunette woman. Picasso stops abruptly and looks up at Roberto.

VOICE OF ROBERTO: Augusto! Picasso! Et voici Miss Frosinone!

PICASSO: Look, there's Roberto ...

Augusto looks up the stairs and immediately his puzzled expression is transmuted to one of excited pleasure.

ROBERTO: Hey, see what a friend I am.

AUGUSTO: Wait! Come on, let's go!

Augusto starts up toward Roberto, beckoning to Picasso to follow. But Picasso does not move.

PICASSO *(calling):* Augusto! Augusto! Where are you going?

Augusto hurries up the stairs, still urging Picasso to follow.

AUGUSTO: Let's go! Come on! Let's go! Come on!

ROBERTO: Hey, Picasso, what are you doing? Hurry up, will you come on? Come on. Look, what a doll!

With ironical, mocking politeness Roberto leads the woman toward Augusto and introduces them, squeezing the woman to his side familiarly.

ROBERTO: This is Mrs. Luigina ... a local gentlewoman ... Mr. Augusto, our spiritual guide. The lady has expressed the desire to take a romantic ride.

WOMAN: Get your hands down, everybody knows me here.

ROBERTO *(ironically):* Excuse me, Ma'am.

He calls to a man with a bicycle who is standing nearby.

ROBERTO: What d'you want? Wait a minute. *(Roberto goes over to the man and hands him some money.)* Here, take this.

A little excited and a little sardonic, Augusto looks the woman up and down in the dim light. She is about forty, badly dressed, and physically unattractive, with rustic animality in her face.

WOMAN: I was sleeping. Hey, I haven't got very much time ... My husband comes home at midnight ...

ROBERTO *(to Augusto and the woman):* Hey, let's go, it's raining!

AUGUSTO *(increasingly excited and amused):* What does your husband do? ...

WOMAN *(shrugging her shoulders):* He works ... *(She is a little intimidated by the elegance of the car.)* What a beautiful car! *(Turning back to the man with the bicycle)* Thanks, Amilcare, then tomorrow ...

Augusto leads the woman to the car, helps her in and starts to follow her; Roberto stops him.

ROBERTO *(bowing to the woman):* Madam! *(To Augusto)* Where are you going? What are you up to? Where are you going?

He bursts out laughing, his eyes shining excitedly for the unexpected adventure. Augusto is completely cured of all melancholy and gets into the car beside the woman.

Roberto closes the door politely and walks around the car to the driver's side. He notices Picasso swaying at the bottom of the stairs as he observes the scene.

ROBERTO: Picassino! ... You go to sleep, get some rest. We'll see you tomorrow morning, eh? So long.

PICASSO: So long.

Roberto gets into the car, slams the door and starts the motor.

The woman can be heard laughing inside the car.

VOICE OF WOMAN: We're jam-packed in here! There's even a radio? Turn it on!

The car drives off.

Picasso, abandoned, looks around bewildered and undecided. A smile of relief illuminates his face after some moments, and he starts off, murmuring.

PICASSO: Home ... Yes, I'll go home ... I'll go home!

He tosses away the coat he had been holding and starts to run.

Piazza in a new section of Rome. Day.

A Sunday morning, toward noon. Church bells toll for the Mass. A large number of people enter and leave the church.

Patrizia, Augusto's daughter, comes out of the church. She is dressed very simply but stylishly.

She looks through the crowd as if expecting someone. After a few moments, Augusto comes up behind her, he too in holiday dress.

AUGUSTO: Did you have to wait long?

PATRIZIA *(turning and smiling at him):* Oh no ... you're right on the dot, Papa.

Augusto takes her hands and gazes at her with pleasure.

AUGUSTO: Let me have a look at you ... You look terrific!

Patrizia, slightly embarrassed, does not know what to answer. Augusto goes over to a flower vendor, takes a flower, and offers it to Patrizia.

PATRIZIA: Oh no, don't bother.

AUGUSTO: Listen. It's a nice day. I have an idea. Why don't we go eat at Monte Mario?

PATRIZIA *(taking her father's arm):* Let's go.

AUGUSTO: Or would you prefer a restaurant in town?

PATRIZIA: It's all the same to me. As long as I'm back home by seven ...

They start off together.

AUGUSTO: Then we'll go to Monte Mario.

Outdoor restaurant on Monte Mario. Day.

Augusto and Patrizia are seated at a table on the restaurant terrace, where a number of other tables are set up and occupied. Patrizia and Augusto have already finished eating.

Patrizia observes her father in silence.

AUGUSTO *(somewhat embarrassed):* I got a little fatter, didn't I?

PATRIZIA: No, you look just fine …

AUGUSTO *(slightly bitter):* You know how old I am? Forty-eight …

PATRIZIA: That's not so old.

Augusto smiles in embarrassment. After another silence he changes the subject.

AUGUSTO: Listen, are you going to finish school?

PATRIZIA: That's just the thing ... I'll have to decide ...

AUGUSTO: What?

PATRIZIA: Decide whether to go on or stop ... It would be four more years in the teacher's high ... and four years is a long time ...

AUGUSTO: What is it? ... You don't like school?

PATRIZIA: Sure I do ... I'd love to go on ... Mama says I should go on, too, but I can't always be a burden to her ...

Augusto is silent for a moment; obviously he has been cut to the quick. He lights a cigarette. Patrizia notices his reaction and is embarrassed.

AUGUSTO: But ... after high school, what would you do?

PATRIZIA: Teach.

AUGUSTO: What?

PATRIZIA: Teach ...

AUGUSTO: And you'd like that? ...

PATRIZIA: Of course ... Actually, I have an idea ... I'd get a job right away, now ... in my spare time ... and I could pay for school that way. A lot of kids do that ... One of my girl friends, for instance, works as a cashier ... and she makes a lot ...

AUGUSTO: But ... how much can a cashier make? ...

PATRIZIA: Well, thirty ... thirty-five ...

AUGUSTO *(surprised):* How much?

PATRIZIA: Thirty-five.

AUGUSTO: Thirty-five? What can you do with thirty-five thousand lire a month ... nobody can live on that!

PATRIZIA: That's more or less what wages are ... A lot of people live on that ... Everybody ...

The waiter arrives with the cake and brandy. Both Augusto and Patrizia are silent for some moments; then, as the waiter leaves, Patrizia continues, as if to sum up.

PATRIZIA: Kids have to earn their own way these days. But actually, it's all just talk ... Just to get a job as a cashier you have to pay a deposit of three hundred thousand lire ... *(Laughing)* and who's got that? ...

Augusto gazes at her in silence; he is taking his sunglasses out of his jacket pocket. A little wristwatch has caught in the glasses.

Patrizia sees it.

She smiles in embarrassment, glancing rapidly at Augusto as if she suddenly guesses that it is a gift for her. She catches herself and goes on with a tone of ostensible, detachment that emphasizes this idea even more.

PATRIZIA: Oh, that's nice looking ... It's really nice.

Augusto has understood her thought; he is embarrassed.

AUGUSTO: You like it? ...

PATRIZIA: Oh, it's beautiful ...

Another moment of embarrassment; Patrizia starts to hand the watch back to Augusto.

AUGUSTO: No, keep it ... it's for you.

PATRIZIA: For me? ... It's too much!

AUGUSTO: No, what do you mean? It's nothing. *(He takes the watch and fastens it onto Patrizia's wrist)* Be careful when you wind it, because ... *(Pause)* it's very delicate ...

PATRIZIA: Thanks, Papa. It's just beautiful.

She holds the watch to her ear, then gazes happily at it.

AUGUSTO *(shouting to the waiter):* Waiter, the bill, please!

Inside a movie theater.

The film on the screen is nearing its end.

An usherette leads Augusto and Patrizia toward a row of seats near the back of the theater.

USHERETTE: Here ... over there. *(Smiles.)* You'll like it better there, I think.

Augusto tips her.

USHERETTE: Thanks.

She goes off as Augusto and Patrizia sit down. Augusto smiles.

AUGUSTO *(softly):* She thought you were my girl friend! *(Patrizia smiles.)* Can you see all right?

PATRIZIA: Oh yes.

They smile at each other. Then, seeming almost to overcome with effort a certain reserve.

AUGUSTO *(with ostensible casualness):* If you want to keep on with your studies ... I'll take care of the deposit.

Patrizia gazes at him in amazement.

AUGUSTO *(as if to minimize his offer, and also to elevate himself in her eyes):* Two or three hundred thousand is nothing for me. I can get that much whenever I want to.

Patrizia is much moved.

PATRIZIA *(simply):* Oh Papa.

Then she suddenly leans over and gives him a kiss. Augusto smiles, somewhat disturbed. The house lights go on; the theater is full. As usual during intermission time, there is a silence that is broken only by the voice of the ice-cream vendor.

VENDOR: Ice cream ... chocolate ... candy ...

AUGUSTO: Want an ice cream?

PATRIZIA: Yes, thanks.

AUGUSTO: Two ice creams. *(As the vendor approaches, Augusto speaks quickly and confidentially)* Don't make any dates for Sunday ... We'll be together, all right? *(Calling again)* Ice cream! ...

A few rows in front of Augusto and Patrizia, a blond equivocal-looking man is combing his hair.

Augusto notices him and starts in fear. He covers his face with his hand in order not to be recognized.

PATRIZIA *(seeing his gesture, worriedly):* What's the matter? Don't you feel well? Hm?

AUGUSTO: No, no, it's nothing.

He continues to cover his face with his hand and to keep an eye on the man. A moment before the house lights go out, the man happens to turn around and recognizes Augusto.

The two men stare at each other. Then Augusto, frightened, rises and with an excuse leaves Patrizia.

AUGUSTO *(to Patrizia):* I'm going to get some cigarettes.

The other man has seen Augusto's move and gets up to follow him.

The two men meet at the back of the theater. Serious, the man plants himself in front of Augusto. Augusto greets him with a pitiful smile.

AUGUSTO *(softly):* Hi! How're things?

MAN *(staring harshly at Augusto, then, with a bleak, menacing tone of voice):* I've been looking for you for six months ...

Augusto smiles, pretending to be perfectly tranquil.

AUGUSTO *(softly):* Can't we talk tomorrow?

These words precipitate the man's wrath.

MAN: Tomorrow? No, we'll talk about it now, now ...

AUGUSTO *(begging for pity, softly):* Listen, please! ...

MAN *(shouting):* Bastard! Coward! I'll wring your neck!

He seizes Augusto's lapel; Augusto tries to free himself.

AUGUSTO *(stammering):* ... You're exaggerating ... Let's go outside and talk calmly ... Not here ...

MAN *(shouting):* We'll talk right here! I'll break your head right here!

The entire audience turns to stare at the two.

VOICES: What's the matter? Shut up? Go fight outside!

Still clutching Augusto's lapel, the man turns for a moment toward a friend who has come up to them.

MAN: Look who's here!

FRIEND *(to Augusto):* Ah, here he is. Fine, fine.

Many of the spectators are on their feet now, protesting loudly: Patrizia has turned to look too.

AUGUSTO: Let's go outside, please!

Theater lobby. Day.

The man and Augusto come out into the lobby. Alarmed, Patrizia follows them.

AUGUSTO: But why do I have to go to Police Headquarters? What have I done?

MAN *(to his friend):* This bastard's still asking what he's done!

FRIEND *(to the man):* Keep calm, or you'll put yourself in the wrong. Better do your talking in Police Headquarters.

MAN *(enraged):* What d'you mean Police Headquarters? I'm going to break this guy's neck!

A policeman hurries toward the little group. The friend sees him and beckons him over.

FRIEND: Ah, here's a cop! Listen, please ...

POLICEMAN: What's happening? What's going on here?

AUGUSTO *(pleading):* Please, let me go now!

The policeman steps between Augusto and the other man.

POLICEMAN: What's going on here?

FRIEND *(to the policeman):* You know what this crook's done? He sold some fake terramycin, my brother almost died!

Patrizia, who has come out into the lobby too, follows the quarrel with increasing trepidation. The man stares violently at Augusto.

MAN: Thief!

FRIEND *(to the man):* That's enough! Take it easy.

POLICEMAN: Hold it! Hold it! That's enough for now!

AUGUSTO *(desperately trying to deny the accusation):* Me, a thief?

POLICEMAN: That's enough, I said!

PATRIZIA: Papa!

Augusto suddenly notices his daughter's presence. He gazes at her, disconcerted and humiliated. He stops resisting and allows himself to be led away.

POLICEMAN: Stop it now! Let's go, come down to Headquarters.

The policeman takes Augusto's arm and pulls him toward the exit. Augusto stops and turns toward Patrizia.

AUGUSTO: Go home.

PATRIZIA *(terrified, standing stock-still):* Papa.

AUGUSTO *(harshly):* Go home!

The group of men starts for the door, as the bystanders murmur.

Outside the movie theater. Day.

Augusto, the man and the policeman come out of the theater and cross the piazza. The small crowd standing in front of the theater watches curiously; a few follow them to try to see what has happened.

Patrizia, too, comes out of the theater and, keeping some little distance behind, follows the group on its way to Police Headquarters.

Outside Police Headquarters. Evening.

It is now evening. Patrizia is sitting on a bench some yards away from the entrance to Police Headquarters.

Augusto comes out, accompanied by two policemen. His eyes are lowered and he holds his hands crossed in front, hidden by his coat. He is handcuffed. Patrizia sees him, rises and follows the scene from behind a tree.

The policemen push Augusto into the paddy wagon. One of them gets in the back with Augusto, the other sits at the wheel.

Patrizia follows them mechanically for a few steps, then stops and bursts into tears.

Outside a prison. Day.

A few months later.

Augusto comes out of the building followed by a guard. Augusto has aged considerably. There is a grayness in his face, a weariness which has left indelible marks.

GUARD: Well, what are you going to do now?

AUGUSTO: I really haven't any idea. Give me a cigarette?

GUARD: Of course! And try not to be a fool again and don't come back in here.

The guard hands Augusto a cigarette and lights it for him.

AUGUSTO: Thanks. So long.

GUARD: So long ... and good luck.

Augusto walks slowly away.

Café Canova, Rome. Day.

The café is crowded; it is the drinking hour.

Riccardo, a friend of Roberto's, is telephoning at the cashier's desk.

RICCARDO *(into telephone):* What are they sequestering? My mother? ... No, no, I'll be out of Rome all week. The

lawyer? They arrested the lawyer! How should I know? No
what ... Ah, I don't know. All right, all right, so long.

*Augusto comes into the café and looks around to see if there is
anyone he knows. Then he goes over to the bar. The barman
recognizes him and smiles briefly.*

AUGUSTO: Hello!

BARMAN: Oh, look who's back! What'll you have? Brandy?

AUGUSTO: No, a Negroni.

BARMAN: Where have you been all this time? Out of town?

AUGUSTO *(without answering):* Has Roberto been in this morning?

BARMAN: Who? That blond guy that's always laughing? He hasn't
been in here for ages.

Riccardo has finished telephoning. He has heard Roberto's name.

RICCARDO *(to Augusto):* Roberto who? Roberto Tucci?

AUGUSTO: Yes.

RICCARDO: Oh, no, he's gone to Milan.

AUGUSTO: Since when?

RICCARDO: It must be three months ago.

AUGUSTO: What's he doing in Milan?

RICCARDO: Ah, he's fixed himself up very nicely. I saw him ... with
an Aurelia sports car ... Yes, yes, it was an Aurelia sports
car.

AUGUSTO *(to the barman):* What about Baron Vargas? Have you
seen him?

BARMAN: I saw him yesterday; today no.

AUGUSTO: But he still comes here, no?

BARMAN: Uh-huh. But less now. The check, please, at the cashier's.

Augusto drinks his Negroni. Riccardo looks significantly at him, as if to size up a prospective accomplice.

Countryside. Day.

A hill road in an almost deserted area.

The black limousine which we saw at the beginning of the film is driving along the road, raising a small cloud of dust. Riccardo, in chauffeur's livery, is at the wheel; the passengers are Augusto, dressed as a prelate, and two other accomplices dressed as priests.

Poor Farmhouse. Outside. Day.

The car stops in the farmyard. The chauffeur gets out, followed by the priest functioning as a secretary. An old man comes out of the farmhouse and approaches the visitors.

The secretary greets the old man, removing his hat.

SECRETARY: Hello!

OLD MAN: Hello!

SECRETARY: Are you Paolo Gozzesi?

OLD MAN: Yes sir.

The elderly priest turns to Augusto, who is getting out of the car.

SECRETARY: It's him, Monsignor. *(To the old man)* We have to have a talk with you about a matter of great importance.

Countryside. Day.

Not far from an abandoned house out in the country, the usual treasure hunt is going on.

The chauffeur, in shirtsleeves, is standing in a hole shoveling out dirt. Waiting at the edge of the hole are the old man, the secretary, and a younger priest who helps the chauffeur dig.

CHAUFFEUR: Oh, there's a bone here!

YOUNGER PRIEST: Monsignor, it's a bone.

CHAUFFEUR: And there's a skull too, look!

Augusto comes over to the hole.

Inside the farmhouse. Day.

In the large dimly lit rustic kitchen someone moves along with great effort, with the help of a pair of crutches. The wooden ends of the crutches tap rhythimically on the brick floor.

The yard door opens and the sudden light shows the invalid to be an extremely pale young girl.

As the door opens, the girl halts, as if ashamed to be found there. She smiles calmly and serenely, but also as if to beg pardon, at the men who are coming back in.

His eyes still partially blinded by the fierce sun outside, Augusto is somewhat struck by the girl. After a moment's hesitation, the chauffeur and the secretary go toward the table and set down the "treasure" and the cloth full of bones.

CHAUFFEUR *(entering):* God how heavy this is, give me a hand, will you? This merits a good cup of coffee.

SECRETARY *(to the girl):* Hello! *(To the chauffeur)* You're right there!

The old peasant comes over to the girl

OLD MAN *(to the girl):* What are you doing out here? Go inside *(To Augusto)* Sorry, Monsignor, this is my daughter, my youngest.

At her father's words, the girl pulls herself along with effort, leaves the kitchen and goes out a side door.

Augusto responds with an embarrassed smile. The chauffeur has begun to search through the pot containing the treasure, pulling out the usual fake jewels and placing them on the table. The secretary is consulting a paper and turns, smiling unctuously at Augusto.

SECRETARY *(marveling):* Monsignor ... look ... it's really a treasure! ...

CHAUFFEUR *(grinning):* Looks like the National Bank!

Augusto gestures slightly to silence them. The two comrades assume an attitude of respectful attention.

Augusto paces up and down, wearily repeating the ritual speech. The old man looks at the objects on the table. A moment's pause.

AUGUSTO: As I told you before ... the treasure is all yours. The deceased left specific orders ... But what you must remember above all is this: you must not say a word to anyone about this. It's a question of murder.

Behind him, the secretary is talking quietly with the old man.

Augusto is still at the window. He closes his eyes. A few moments later, the secretary's voice rouses him.

SECRETARY: Monsignor ... *(Augusto turns.)* There's a little difficulty ... The gentleman here hasn't got enough to cover the entire amount for the Masses ... He seems to have only ... How much do you have, how much do you have?

OLD MAN: Three hundred fifty thousand lire.

SECRETARY: Three hundred fifty thousand. What should we do?

AUGUSTO *(assuming an irritated tone of voice):* It doesn't matter! We're not here to do business, after all! Let him give whatever he has, and for the rest, you can come back, or I'll explain to His Eminence!

OLD MAN: You see, I've saved up this money because tomorrow I was going to the fair to buy an ox; it would make the work so much easier. I have to think about putting something aside, you know? Not for me, but for those two poor girls. One works for me like a man, but the other one, poor thing, is paralyzed, and when I die who'll take care of her?

SECRETARY: Oh come along now! You're unjust; don't talk that way! The good Lord never abandons anyone. You see what Providence has seent you? A treasure! *(To Augusto)* Isn't that so, Monsignor?

The chauffeur is holding some of the objects of the treasure.

CHAUFFEUR *(chuckling)*: Ah, I'd sure like to have the bad luck this poor peasant has!

AUGUSTO: The Lord never abandons his creatures. Have you got the money with you?

OLD MAN: Yes, I have it right here. Here, please ...

The old man takes a roll of ten-thousand lire bills from his pocket and hands it to the secretary. Everyone watches with the greatest attention, in silence.

SECRETARY *(to Augusto)*: Oh! Monsignor!

Augusto takes the roll of bills. The younger priest steps in deferentially.

YOUNGER PRIEST: It's getting late, Monsignor. His Eminence will be waiting for us at five.

SECRETARY: Yes, that's true, we ought to leave. *(To the old man)* Excuse us. Goodbye for now.

Augusto moves toward the door, followed by his accomplices and the old man. As they come out in the farmyard, the mother appears in another doorway and approaches Augusto.

MOTHER: Monsignor! Monsignor! Forgive me. Do something for me. Talk a little bit with my daughter?

AUGUSTO: But ... I can't ...

MOTHER: Please, Monsignor. Just for a minute.

AUGUSTO *(turning to his three companions):* Wait a minute for me.

MOTHER: Thank you, thank you so much. But don't tell her I asked you to.

Augusto and the mother go toward the back of the house.

The girl is sitting on a chair against the wall. Augusto and the mother approach her.

MOTHER *(to the daughter):* Look, Monsignor wanted to say goodbye to you. *(To Augusto)* I'll go get you a chair, Monsignor.

AUGUSTO: No, no, I'm leaving right away. *(The girl starts to get up, but Augusto stays her with a gesture.)* No, no, Sit down, sit down.

The tender good-nature of the young paralytic helps him overcome his embarrassment despite himself.

AUGUSTO: What's your name?

SUSANNA: Susanna.

A silence ensues; Augusto does not know what to say. Then he plunges in.

AUGUSTO: You must have faith in God, you know, my dear girl. I understand, it's a terrible thing for you, but we must resign ourselves to His will. This is a vale of tears, and each of us bears his own cross.

The girl has not noticed the conventional tone of Augusto's phrases. For her they are not conventional words. She smiles.

SUSANNA *(smiling):* I know, and I don't complain ... *(She looks down at the ground and continues seriously:)* If it weren't for them ...

AUGUSTO (looking at her in astonishment): What do you mean, "them"?

SUSANNA: If I weren't a burden for my family, I wouldn't care at all.

AUGUSTO: What, in your condition, you worry about them?

The mother comes back outside and stands over Susanna.

MOTHER *(moved):* She always has this idea, Monsignor. She always has this idea of being a burden, my daughter! But why do you talk that way? And it's not true at all, Monsignor; she's always working. She can calculate better than a teacher. And embroidery: look at what kind of work she does.

The mother bends down to take the piece of embroidery that the girl has been sewing. Susanna humbly tries to dissuade her.

MOTHER: Let me. Show Monsignor. Look, look what beautiful work!

The mother hands the embroidery frame to the embarrassed Augusto.

AUGUSTO *(hesitating, to the mother):* But ... has she always been like this?

MOTHER: No, Monsignor, from when she was nine years old, it's polio.

The mother bends down to kiss her daughter's hair, then goes off some few yards to weep.

SUSANNA: Mama, Mama, go back inside.

AUGUSTO: And how old are you?

SUSANNA *(smiling):* Eighteen.

Augusto is touched by the girl's smiling, serene acceptance.

AUGUSTO *(as if to himself):* Nine years!

SUSANNA: Oh, but I'm fine here, you know? I sit here with my embroidery, I listen to music ... I feel like a queen ... *(She throws her head back and laughs heartily. She points at the countryside.)* For my sister life really is hard. She's been down in the field working since four this morning.

AUGUSTO *(almost puzzled):* But wouldn't you want to get better?

The girl is startled. Her eyes search Augusto's as if to discover the reason for such a question.

SUSANNA: But ... it's impossible. No ... it would take a miracle ...

AUGUSTO: Miracles sometimes happen.

SUSANNA: Ah, yes, I know!

AUGUSTO: You believe in them?

SUSANNA *(smiling):* Certainly I do.

AUGUSTO: Why?

SUSANNA *(laughing):* ... I don't know why, but I do! *(She suddenly turns serious and continues, following her own thoughts.)* My misfortune has made me find God. I'm always happy, even when I feel so bad I could die.

She bursts into tears, then smiles again, looking at Augusto, who hesitantly and uncomfortably hands back the sewing.

AUGUSTO: This embroidery is really beautiful.

Then he abruptly starts to take his leave.

SUSANNA *(apprehensively):* You're leaving, Monsignor?

AUGUSTO: I have to go now. I have to go. *(As if drained by the painful truth of the conversation, Augusto begins to speak in a sincere tone of voice.)* You don't need me. You're much better off than a lot of other people. Our life ... the life of so many people I know has nothing beautiful in it. You're not losing much, you don't need me, I have nothing to give you.

Augusto goes off. Susanna picks up her crutches.

SUSANNA *(weeping):* No, Monsignor, wait, don't go away. *(She catches up with him, takes his hand and bends to kiss it, sobbing.)* Pray for me! Pray for me!

Overcome and irritated by Susanna's gesture of heartrending devotion, Augusto pulls his hand away almost roughly.

AUGUSTO: Stop it!

He goes off.

Country road. Day.

The black car speeds back along the road, which winds through a solitary, wild landscape.

Inside the car. Day.

Inside the car, Augusto—his expression fairly strained—observes his companion, asleep beside him, with some disgust.

Country road. Day.

Vargas' little Fiat is parked on the side of the road. The landscape is rough and lonely. A rocky hillside falls steeply away to the valley below.

The black car pulls up behind the small Fiat. Vargas comes toward the car, stuffing his newspaper back in his pocket.

The young man in chauffeur's uniform opens the front door and gets out.

CHAUFFEUR: Why didn't you dig a little deeper, this morning? Boy you really made me sweat ...

VARGAS *(opening the back door):* So? ... How did it go?

The secretary gets out on Vargas' side. Augusto opens the other door and slips out in silence.

SECRETARY: Three hundred fifty thousand. We could have got more. But that was all they had in the house and we thought it was better to leave.

VARGAS: You did right. I certainly didn't expect you at this hour.

Augusto, at the back of the car, is rapidly removing his cross and red ribbon; his face is tense, and he speaks curtly to the other two.

AUGUSTO: Who's got the keys?

SECRETARY: He has. *(To the chauffeur)* Give him the keys.

The chauffeur takes the keys from his pocket and tosses them to Augusto. He is whistling a tune.

SECRETARY *(to the chauffeur):* What's the name of that tune?

CHAUFFEUR: The Menga Symphony.

Augusto opens the trunk and deposits the cross, the hat, and the red ribbon inside. He begins to remove his priestly robes with the same rapid movements, his face still strained.

The secretary comes to join him, and places his own soutane in the trunk.

SECRETARY: And the bottle of brandy?

CHAUFFEUR: I drank the brandy. I worked like a dog there, you could get pneumonia that way.

The secretary takes his coat and hat from the trunk and dons them. In the background the younger priest, now in civilian dress, is dancing around pretending to box.

SECRETARY: I've got a pain here since this morning. I told my wife so, too. She says to me: You work too hard. And it's true.

CHAUFFEUR: Antonio, where's the bottle? Oh, here it is.

The chauffeur pours water from the flask into the car's radiator.

VARGAS *(to the chauffeur):* What are you doing with that bottle?

CHAUFFEUR: What d'you mean, what am I doing, I'm putting in water. I had to come all the way uphill in second. If you don't decide to junk this car, you're in for trouble.

VARGAS: Who's got the money?

SECRETARY: Augusto has. Augusto's got it.

Augusto, who is knotting his tie, hesitates for an instant; then, grim-faced, he explodes.

AUGUSTO: You really are a bunch of scum ... I don't have the money, I didn't take it. *(His companions freeze and stare at him in silence, not understanding.)* How could anyone take it? You bastards, then you'd steal from your own mothers, would you?

YOUNGER BOY *(calling from a distance):* Oh, what are you saying anyway?!

AUGUSTO *(to Vargas):* I couldn't do it, Vargas, I just didn't have the gall to do it. He was a poor old coot with a paralytic daughter. He works so she won't end up in a home ...

VARGAS *(curtly):* Augusto, don't make me laugh. *(To the chauffeur)* What's he saying?

SECRETARY: Augusto, I saw you myself when you took it.

VOICE OF AUGUSTO: And I gave it back.

YOUNGER BOY: When did you give it back?

AUGUSTO *(raising his voice):* I gave it back, understand?

Augusto puts on his jacket and removes his coat and hat from the trunk, under the menacing stares of his accomplices.

Vargas comes slowly over to Augusto.

VARGAS *(in a sly, somewhat sinister tone):* Augusto ... You're the biggest bastard I ever knew. Look, you had three hundred and fifty thousand in your hand and you let them go—you?!

Augusto's eyes meet Vargas'.

AUGUSTO *(simply, in a tone of sincerity):* Did I ever try to con you? *(After a silence, shrugging his shoulders))* I tell you I couldn't do it.

He notices that the secretary has taken his priest's cassock from the trunk and is searching it.

AUGUSTO *(aggressively):* There's no point looking there. It's not there.

SECRETARY: We'll see if I don't find the money.

AUGUSTO: You were all in the car, but I was talking with the girl. A poor sick kid nailed to that chair for nine years now, and knows she'll never get better. She looks you in the eyes, she kisses your hand, she asks you to pray for her. I'd like to see what you would have done, if you're real men. I have a daughter and I couldn't do it.

VARGAS: Everything down the drain. Work, risk of prison! ... Have you gone crazy?!

AUGUSTO: Can't I have a conscience too?

VARGAS: That would be something new! *(Pause)* But is it really true?

AUGUSTO: I swear to you. Let's go.

He starts to get back into the car, but the younger man stops him roughly.

YOUNGER BOY: Just a minute. Everybody trusts each other, everybody's friends. All these fine speeches, I'm even touched, but I don't believe it. Let's have a look!

He starts to lay hands on Augusto to frisk him. Augusto thrusts his hand away and steps back.

AUGUSTO: Leave me alone! And don't you lay a hand on me, you!

The chauffeur takes Augusto by the arm in feigned friendliness.

CHAUFFEUR: Augusto, what are you trying to say? Come on. Augusto, I was there, too, don't you remember, I was there, too, with you. I saw you take it. Why are you trying to kid us? Thanks a lot, make us laugh, but now it's enough, it's enough now.

AUGUSTO: But I don't have the money!

The younger boy jumps Augusto from behind, immobilizing his arms as the chauffeur tries to search him.

VARGAS: Frisk him!

AUGUSTO *(slipping away):* But I don't have it!

CHAUFFEUR: And if you don't have it, what do you care, let us see.

AUGUSTO: Let me alone!

Augusto hurls the chauffeur to the ground.

CHAUFFEUR: You hurt my elbow, goddam you. *(To the others)* He's got the money, he's got it on him!!!

AUGUSTO *(panting, challenging them):* Come on, come on! You don't scare me!

VARGAS: You! You think it'll end like this!

Augusto bends down to retrieve his hat and just at that moment the younger boy leaps on him again. A violent battle ensues; the young man punches him repeatedly, with brutality.

VOICES: You filthy scum! You want to cheat me! On your knees you have to bring it to me, in your teeth!

Augusto manages to free himself and starts to run down the road. Vargas throws a rock at him, which misses.

VARGAS: I'll kill you! I'll kill you!

Augusto suddenly turns off the road and heads down the steep, rocky hillside.

The other three follow him; Vargas is farther behind.

They halt briefly to pick up and hurl rocks at Augusto.

Augusto races down the hillside, stopping only to throw some rocks back at his pursuers. One rock catches him on the forehead.

With a suffocated cry, Augusto falls to the ground, hitting his back against a boulder.

Augusto lies on the ground, moving very little and moaning weakly. There is no blood on him.

AUGUSTO: My back ... my back ... *(The two younger pursuers reach him in a moment. Panting, they immediately proceed to frisk him.)* Hold it! Hold it! My back! My back!

Vargas and the secretary hurry down the cliff and near them.

The younger boy emits a soft exclamation of triumph.

He removes a large roll of bills from one of Augusto's shoes.

YOUNGER BOY: Here it is! He had it in his shoe. This bastard!

For a moment only the panting of the men and Augusto's moaning can be heard.

Augusto tries to prevent them from taking the money.

AUGUSTO *(his voice choking):* It's mine, I need it, leave it alone!

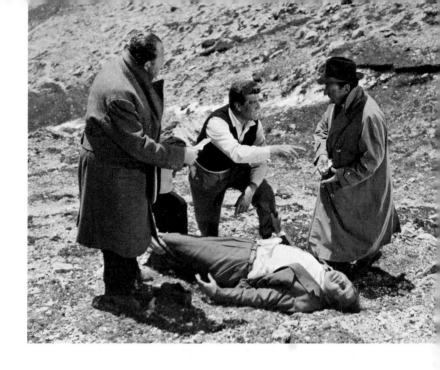

The two men continue to search Augusto. The chauffeur shouts to Vargas:

CHAUFFEUR: He's got it all on him! All of it!

The secretary reaches them and stops a few feet away.

SECRETARY *(panting):* Where's the money? Where is it?...

The chauffeur gives him the roll of money he has found.

CHAUFFEUR: Here it is! Count it.

SECRETARY *(spitting at Augusto):* You bastard! *(He shows the money to Vargas, who has just come up.)* Here's the money. *(To Augusto)* Damned sonuvabitch!

Vargas takes the money from the secretary and from the younger boy, glances in furious disdain at Augusto and exclaims in a choked voice:

VARGAS: The paralytic daughter! The paralytic daughter! *(Then carried away by his ferocious fury, he kicks Augusto violently. Augusto screams; Vargas kicks him two or three times more, violently.)* You're finished working with me ... In Rome you won't work with anybody again ever. *(To the others)* He'd almost convinced me ... this crook!

Augusto moans, more deeply and hoarsely now, then remains silent, his eyes staring blankly and his mouth contracted.

Vargas starts to go back up to the road.

VARGAS *(to the younger men):* Come on ... Leave him, he'll manage by himself. *(Turning to shout back at Augusto)* And I'll give you the rest in Rome! That bastard.

Augusto, stretched out on the ground, turns his eyes slowly toward them, with a gleam of terrified bewilderment in his eyes.

AUGUSTO *(his voice choked):* Vargas ... I'm hurt...

VARGAS: Screw you! *(To the others)* Come on, let's go.

He starts up the hill; the secretary and the younger boy follow; the chauffeur, standing beside Augusto, jokes cruelly.

CHAUFFEUR: See what kind of friends you have? They're leaving you out here to enjoy the countryside.

VARGAS *(calling back to Augusto):* You've done a really goofy thing. The goofiest thing you ever did in your whole life.

AUGUSTO: Vargas, Vargas ... I'm hurt! Take me home ...

CHAUFFEUR: Who're you trying to kid? Who are you kidding?

The chauffeur starts up the hill. Augusto is alone.

His face is bathed in sweat; he tries to call out again, but his voice comes out only very weakly.

AUGUSTO: Vargas! Vargas ... don't leave me here! I'm hurt, I'm really hurt bad ... I can't move!

No one answers him.

With a desperate effort he tries to lift his head up so that his voice will reach the others, but he falls back with a groan and a grimace of pain.

He lies there gasping and half-crazed. He raises his head again, shouting in the same choked voice:

AUGUSTO *(to the chauffeur):* Riccardo! Riccardo, listen ... you're my friend...

CHAUFFEUR: Of course!

AUGUSTO: Don't leave me here! You're young ... I can teach you ... I can teach you ... *(Grimaces with pain.)* I can teach you so many things.

VOICE OF CHAUFFEUR: What do you want to teach me, to be a bastard like you?!

AUGUSTO: I have some money hidden ... we'll split it, but don't leave me here! Vargas! ... I know you're there ... What do you want? ... You want to scare me? ... That's enough now! ... Vargas! Vargas! *(Screams.)*

In the silence, a motor is suddenly heard starting up and fading into the distance.

Augusto listens with desperate tenseness. A second motor is heard starting up; the second one too fades away into the distance.

AUGUSTO *(screaming):* Vargas! Vargas!

He gasps for breath, tries to pull himself up, to shout with another desperate effort.

A moan escapes his lips, his eyes cloud over and he falls back in a faint.

Augusto is slowly coming back to consciousness. He opens his eyes and looks around almost in astonishment, almost as if he had forgotten where he was and why. The sun is still hot, although it is now far down toward the mountains. Augusto's face is bathed in sweat.

Perhaps without being aware of it, he murmurs, as if wishing to reassure himself:

AUGUSTO: Of course they'll be back ... And what if I die? No, I can't die like this! But ... *(A lacerating pain wracks him.)* if I die? ... *(He gasps in growing terror, and shouts:)* Help! Help!

His eyes stray through the air toward the sun, which is about to set behind the purple mountains. He gazes at the sky, illuminated by the sunset.

AUGUSTO: I knew it would end like this ... I always knew it. And if I manage to get over this ... I'm never going to support anybody ... that's why I'm dying...

Night has fallen. Suddenly the sound of a motor can be heard coming up the road. Augusto does not notice it immediately, but as the noise becomes stronger and clearer, he is suddenly roused.

His eyes come to life again; he raises his head and listens tensely. The noise of the motor comes closer. It is clearly a truck.

Augusto pulls himself a little further up. He turns his eyes up toward the road, which cannot be seen.

Now the truck passes directly above him, but continues on its way.

AUGUSTO: Vargas ... But ... I don't remember...

His head falls back to the ground in infinite despair.

AUGUSTO *(weeping):* Oh, Patrizia, my baby girl!...

It is almost dawn. Augusto lies immobile on the ground in the growing light of the rising sun.

Then he moves, raises his head slightly and with a tremendous effort manages to turn over on his stomach. A stream of blood pours from

his mouth and for a moment his dirty, sweaty face looks relieved.

AUGUSTO: That's better ... I can ... I can ... I can...

He bites his lips to keep from screaming; gasping for breath, he tries to pull himself up the hillside.

His face is contracted by pain and desperation.

Augusto continues to drag himself up the hillside, as if he had decided to play all for all. He grasps at the gravel, slips back, starts up again.

He gasps ever more deeply. He is no longer weeping; all is silent about him.

Augusto has now reached the edge of the road.

In the silence, children's voices are suddenly heard; they seem unreal, but they are real. Footsteps can be heard.

VOICE OF LITTLE GIRL: Oh! ... Come here!...

From the ground, Augusto slowly turns his already-dim gaze toward those voices. Some children are coming along the road with two peasant women. The little group passes by Augusto without seeing him, and continues on its way.

Augusto stares without understanding; then a grimace, which seems to be a smile, appears on his bloody face and relaxes his features. His salvation is attained. His lips move; his head nods slightly.

AUGUSTO: Wait for me ... I'm coming ... I'm coming with you...

Still with that shadow of a smile, he finally falls prostrate, his face half-crushed into the ground.

He is dead.

THE END

The Temptations of
Doctor Antonio

Credits

CARLO PONTI presents

BOCCACCIO 70
scherzo in four acts
conceived by CESARE ZAVATTINI

ACT II
FEDERICO FELLINI
THE TEMPTATIONS OF DOCTOR ANTONIO

Written by:	Federico Fellini
	Ennio Flaiano
	Tullio Pinelli
Collaborators:	B. Rondi
	B. Parise
Set designer:	P. Zuffi
Editing:	L. Catozzo
Photography:	Otello Martelli
Music:	Nino Rota
Cast:	
Mazzuolo:	Peppino de Filippo
Anita:	Anita Ekberg

The E.U.R. World's Fair zone in Rome. Day.

The E.U.R. quarter on a radiant spring day. Freshness, renewal, and purity are in the pleasantly warm air along the boulevards, among the colossal marble buildings, and down along the avenue leading to the lake.

The blast of a cannon marks midday.

The city church bells peal in a distant concerto dominated by the great bell of St. Peter's and joined by the higher-pitched bells of the nearby E.U.R. Church.

A chic, rainbow-garbed crowd is entering the church for noon Mass.

The sidewalk cafés under the arcades of the great white buildings are filled with people sitting at the tables and taking in the warm sun. There is a constant movement of cars pulling up and departing. A small voice begins to speak, now jestingly, now childishly indignant, frequently stumbling over the more difficult words:

LITTLE VOICE: I'd love to live in Rome. 'Specially now it's spring. I have such a great time. I wander around on foot, or hitch a ride, or take a bli-blicycle...Soon's they see me, all the women start bawling. They're so happy. They pick me up, they call me a little rascal; "Just look at the cute little fellow!"; "Aren't you ashamed?". But there's one guy that really has it in for me. He really pre-propresecutes me! Some day I'll end up losing my temper and then he'll be in for it! But why, I ask you? I just fool around sometimes. Little games. Can't a person even fool around, I ask you?

No they can't. He takes everything so seriously; he's always looking on the black side of things. But after all, if I wasn't around to keep people's spirits up, the world would be just a cata-catra-catatrastrophe!

A couple is kissing inside a car nearby. Up in the sky a tiny plane is skywriting "Happy Easter."

Accompanied by a priest, a group of American boarding-school girls is blithely and coquettishly descending a marble stairway. They are wearing light spring dresses and all are laughing gaily.

In an open lot nearby, bordered by a number of new apartment buildings, a crew of workmen are up on ladders plastering the paper strips of an advertisement on an enormous billboard. The billboard stands about six yards off the ground, and has a display surface of about ten by twenty yards. The few sheets already hung do not as yet give an idea of what the ad will represent: only two bare feet are visible, themselves longer than the workmen now gluing them on.

Preceded by the referees' car, a group of amateur bicycle racers speeds by toward the highway leading to the sea. The billboard crew cheers them on and comments jokingly.

Now the American girls applaud the cyclists.

Immediately after the racers, an automobile in the shape of a giant toothpaste tube pulls up in front of the girls. The two young men inside call out to invite the girls for a ride. But since no one takes up their offer, they depart with an air of injured superiority.

Two elephants lumber across one of the avenues, led by their driver.

Off in a meadow, two lovers are kissing. As the Little Voice announces "Here he comes now," a photograph of Dr. Mazzuolo blocks the couple from view.

LITTLE VOICE: Here he comes now ...

The photograph shows Dr. Mazzuolo in morning dress, bending to kiss the hand of someone whose face is cut off by the edge of the photograph.

LITTLE VOICE: Hold it, maybe this doesn't give a very good idea of him. This one's better...

Another photograph of Mazzuolo blocks out the first; it shows him face on, standing before a microphone, speaking with great agitation.

LITTLE VOICE *(hesitantly):* He isn't even so bad looking ... Well ... that is...

A third photograph of Mazzuolo now appears, showing him obsequiously following a VIP, with a leather briefcase under his arm.

LITTLE VOICE: That is, I mean there are a lot of worse-looking people ... That's what makes me so mad ... Here he is ... Do you think that's any way ... He's a menace to the plu-plublic...

Boulevard on the outskirts of the city. Night.

At the wheel of a medium-sized Fiat, Dr. Mazzuolo drives along a wide and lonely unlit boulevard on the outskirts of the city. Ten or twelve cars are parked along the walls and under the trees, with only their parking lights on.

Dr. Mazzuolo's expression is one of disdain and disgust. He begins to sound his horn energetically and flashes his brights into the parked cars. He leans over to the right-hand window as he passes by.

DR. MAZZUOLO *(shouting):* For shame! ... For shame!...

As Dr. Mazzuolo's car drives off, a childish giggle can be heard.

Seaside resort. Day.

The little voice goes on:

LITTLE VOICE: And you haven't seen anything yet ... You want to see what he did last summer?

A crowd of vacationers and tourists promenade along the sea at a fashionable resort enjoying its high season.

A very beautiful woman, evidently a foreigner, comes through the crowd escorted by several young men. Her costume is particularly close-fitting.

Mazzuolo, in a white suit and straw hat, stops suddenly as he notices her heading in his direction. When the woman, unaware of the danger, is but a few paces away, he steps into her path and lashes out at her with a couple of slaps.

After a moment's astonishment, the young men accompanying the woman falls upon Mazzuolo, and a noisy fist fight ensues.

The little voice is heard giggling once again.

Theater. Inside. Night.

On the stage of a burlesque theater, three splendid-looking chorus girls are performing a dance number; their charms are not excessively concealed by the feathers and sequins of their multicolored costumes.

Burlesque music.

Down in the orchestra, where the audience is enjoying the show to the utmost, Mazzuolo suddenly stands up from his seat, raising his arm aloft and shouts something that cannot be heard over the music. Those seated nearby turn to gaze at him in surprise, and everyone gradually becomes aware of the little man who continues to shout at the top of his lungs.

On stage, the dancers look down into the orchestra, turn to gaze at each other in consternation, and miss their steps. Other members of the troupe peer out from behind the curtain. The orchestra music grinds to a halt.

Standing in the orchestra, the wrathful Mazzuolo shouts.

MAZZUOLO: Stop it! ... I protest! ... Commissioner! ... This business has got to stop now!...

E.U.R. Church. Inside. Day.

Now wearing an appropriately somber suit, Mazzuolo passes through the pews during the elegant noon Mass, taking up pious offerings in a green velvet purse.

E.U.R. Outside. Day.

The crowd pours out of church at the end of mass. Mazzuolo is among the last to leave. The weather is very hot, and he wipes the sweat from his brow before coming down the steps and starting down the avenue. He walks rapidly, his face grave and his eyes turned to the ground.

But his attention is instinctively attracted by something unusual. He lifts his eyes and comes to a sudden stop with an expression of horror on his face.

The billboard crew has now finished its labors: an enormous Anita Ekberg, in a low-cut, skin-tight evening gown, has been plastered across the skies. She is reclining on a couch, holding a glass filled with a white liquid; a disturbingly ambiguous smile illuminates her face as she gazes out at the beholder.

The gigantic lettering on the sign reads: DRINK MORE MILK.

Mazzuolo remains glued to the spot: obviously the colossal image of that woman has thrown him into the greatest turmoil. He stares at the billboard in fascination, unable to tear his eyes away.

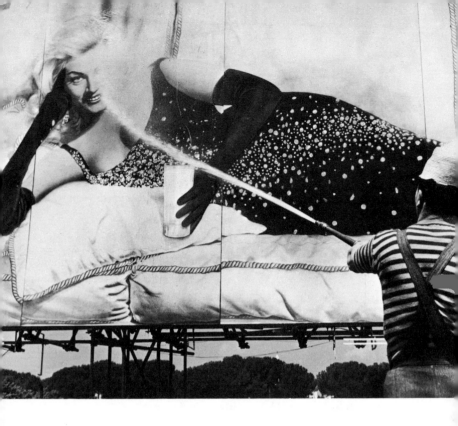

Anita continues to stare back at him from her couch with her provocative smile.

Mazzuolo finally breaks out of his trance. He looks about with an expression of extreme disgust and wrath.

Not far from the billboard and from Mazzuolo, the workmen are loading their ladders and equipment back on the truck. They smoke and tiredly exchange remarks.

Seeing them getting back in the truck, Mazzuolo waves to catch their attention, then hurries over to them.

MAZZUOLO: Excuse me … excuse me, are you leaving that sign just like that?

The workmen look blankly at him, without curiosity. The two drivers watch from the cab.

MAZZUOLO: This is a public area ... open to everybody ... everybody comes here ... children ... ladies ... adolescents ... even old people...

The workmen have still not understood. One of them looks first at his companions and then answers, with mixed deference and aggressiveness:

FIRST WORKMAN: It's a sign. Where else should it go? In some cellar?

MAZZUOLO *(kindly, but upset):* No, I'm sorry, look here a minute. This is just a job for you, I understand ... You're just doing your jobs. But there are some responsibilities here too ... moral responsibilities ... This is an obviously immoral sign. Obscene! You can't deny that! *(Smiling)* Maybe you didn't realize that! But just take a look at it.

The workmen look at the sign. One of them slowly explains to the others:

SECOND WORKMAN: He says it's against morals.

The workmen conscientiously look at the sign once again. One cocks his head like a painter admiring a canvas.

Mazzuolo expounds the problem.

MAZZUOLO: The position! We're all men, we know about certain things ... The position speaks for itself. Provocative ... voluptuous ... sensuous! ... The way the dress *accentuates;* it leaves no doubt ... *(Pointing to an apartment building)* Besides, that's my house right there! You're putting it right under my window! Intolerable! Let's be reasonable! I have a family, I have a wife...

A third workman tries to wind matters up; his tone is reassuring but his expression is of absolute indifference.

THIRD WORKMAN: You're perfectly right, sir. But there's nothing we can do about it now. The police have approved it.

He motions to the driver as if to say "Let's get out of here."

MAZZUOLO: No, no! Just a minute. Do something. Look, in a way, you're accomplices! Do something, cover it up, hide part of it. I'll help you! You could put a little paper over it here, and here ... and here ... I could even contribute something, a little something, for this extra work ...

SECOND WORKMAN: No, no, sir. Can't be done!

FOURTH WORKMAN *(in an even more energetic tone of voice):* You crazy or something? Come on, let's get out of here!

The driver races the engine. Mazzuolo is about to place himself in front of the truck to prevent its departure, but it gets the jump on him and he has to leap back to avoid being hit. The truck drives off.

Alone, Mazzuolo grimaces wrathfully and starts for his own building, about a hundred yards away, darting hate-filled glances back at the sign as he goes.

DOORMAN *(in a servile manner):* Good afternoon, Dr. Mazzuolo.

MAZZUOLO: Good afternoon.

He stops for a moment before entering the building, as if to elicit solidarity from the doorman. The latter does not understand and smiles hesitantly and obsequiously at him before following Mazzuolo's gaze to the billboard out in the lot. Believing he has correctly interpreted Mazzuolo's glances, the doorman flashes him a smile of arch complicity.

DOORMAN: Great stuff, eh?

MAZZUOLO *(enraged, curtly):* This is sheer persecution! It can't be tolerated any more!

He enters the building. Disconcerted, the doorman has instantly swallowed his grin.

Out on the boulevard, the two elephants saunter by again.

Mazzuolo's apartment. Bathroom. Day.

Mazzuolo is showering. He soaps himself hurriedly, his face glowering. As he leaves the shower, naked and dripping, he notices that the billboard can be seen through the open window.

He puts on his glasses to have a better look.

Anita gazes at him with a provocative and—given the situation—an extremely significant smile.

Disturbed and frowning, Mazzuolo rapidly girds his waist with a towel and slams the window shut.

Mazzuolo's apartment. Living room. Day.

Mazzuolo is at the dinner table with his wife, a woman still fairly young but already fading. She is pregnant; she eats slowly, and has the bearing of a victim.

Mazzuolo eats nervously, stopping now and then to look out the window facing him. As the curtain sways back and forth in the breeze, it alternately reveals and blocks out the view, which includes, far below, the enormous billboard. At last Mazzuolo can stand it no longer; he gets up and closes the window.

WIFE *(whiningly):* Paolo, the heat's suffocating! ... *(She turns to the maid, who is serving dinner)* ... Open it just a little...

The girl opens the window again just as Mazzuolo sits down. The curtain begins to blow back and forth again, alternately revealing and concealing Anita Ekberg's enormous smile before Mazzuolo's grim eyes.

Overcome by wrath, Mazzuolo suddenly swallows something the wrong way and sputters.

Mazzuolo's apartment. Study. Day.

Mazzuolo's large, well-lit study has the air of the sacristy about it. There are a great number of leather-bound books, religious paintings, ugly bric-a-brac, a typewriter and a desk with a tape recorder and telephone.

Mazzuolo is telephoning. Now and then he glances out the window at Anita's billboard.

MAZZUOLO *(on the telephone):* Perhaps you don't quite get the picture, because you haven't seen it for yourself. But *I* have to look at it! Oh, yes indeed. There is a law that prohibits obscene publications. I'm invoking that law ... Yes, yes, yes ... The government has the duty ... I've done it in other cases. A formal protest ... You, in the meantime, pass the word on to your superiors right away ... What d'you mean, no one's there? Tomorrow? Why tomorrow? Today! It's an extremely urgent matter. *(Sweating, upset, insistent, Mazzuolo battles over the telephone.)* Which office? ... Yes. Put him on.

Mazzuolo's apartment. Bedroom. Day.

Mazzuolo is out on the balcony, observing. He looks in turn at the billboard, taking in all the details, and at the reactions of the passers-by. Only a few people are out at this siesta hour: a group of boys who race by on their bikes without even noticing the sign, a couple of street sweepers, four nuns.

Mazzuolo arrives at a decision. He slips his jacket on rapidly and rushes out of the apartment.

Commendatore's home. Entrance. Day.

Mazzuolo is waiting in the entrance hall, where he can hear the voices of people in the dining room carrying on a lively conversation. The Commendatore hurries in, his superficial courteousness scarcely concealing his obvious annoyance.

COMMENDATORE: Good afternoon ... What's on your mind, Dr. Mazzuolo? ... Do forgive me if I don't ask you in, but I have dinner guests, and we were just ... *(He gestures to say, "Just going to sit down.")* But if it's something urgent ... Tell me...

MAZZUOLO: It's a question of principle ... I know I can count on your understanding and your support...

At this preamble, the Commendatore becomes diffident as well as vexed.

COMMENDATORE: Oh, you mustn't think I have so very much power. Tell me what it's all about.

MAZZUOLO: Perhaps you haven't noticed what's happened here ... right under our windows.

COMMENDATORE *(beginning to be alarmed):* No.

MAZZUOLO: I'm at a loss to describe it. You can judge for yourself. If you'll just take a look out here a minute...

Alarmed but still diffident, the Commendatore goes over to the window and opens it.

COMMENDATORE: What's happened? *(He looks out, fails to understand but feigns.)* Ah! … *(He squints and takes out his glasses.)* What's it say? Sorry, without my glasses I can't…

MAZZUOLO: "Drink More Milk." But that's not the point.

COMMENDATORE *(reading):* "Drink More Milk" … Yes…

He turns to look questioningly at Mazzuolo.

MAZZUOLO: It's not the slogan … Look … look at the picture. It's absolutely intolerable.

COMMENDATORE: Yes, it certainly does block the view … But when they begin to build it'll be even worse…

MAZZUOLO: The picture! Just look at it a minute … Unfortunately, we've had to get used to an escalation of obscenity, but there's a limit!

The Commendatore gazes at the billboard with renewed interest.

COMMENDATORE: Ah ... Yes, yes, yes ... Yes ... It certainly isn't ... It's fairly ... Actually ... *(Suddenly lighting up)* Anita Ekberg! *(He spreads his arms and attempts to ease Mazzuolo toward the door.)* The times we live in, dear sir! But it can't be helped...

Mazzuolo resists stubbornly, although he is ill at ease and deferent to the important personage.

MAZZUOLO: I take the position that something must be done ... We must react. Rebel! The decent people must unite. And I assure you that we can get results ... Every time I've protested, I've had some success ... We have to be courageous...

A gorgeous maid, looking like a caricature in her skimpy skintight uniform, enters the room to announce discretely that dinner is ready.

She gestures. As soon as Mazzuolo sees her, he draws back in astonishment.

COMMENDATORE *(to the maid):* Yes, right away.

Mazzuolo rushes even more insistently through the climax of his speech.

MAZZUOLO: I've already telephoned. The authorization can be withdrawn ... A protest ... with your authoritative support ... It would be important to act fairly quickly. So many people go by here ... children ... young girls ... It's like poison. Every hour that goes by, the moral damage is compounded ... There's not a minute to lose.

COMMENDATORE *(now almost pushing him toward the door):* Yes, yes, yes, you're perfectly right ... Morally, I agree with you. But if it's been authorized ... Evidently it was within the law

... As you said, we've seen worse than this, unfortunately ... *(Impatient, already almost irritated, he snatches up several magazines from a table.)* Look ... look here! Look at this one!

MAZZUOLO: But this one is fully dressed!

COMMENDATORE: That's just the point! Look at this foot. This naked foot peeping out from under the dress, like a little hand waving ... beckoning...

MAZZUOLO: But there's no comparison! Look at that ... *(He takes the Commendatore back to the window and points at the sign.)* Look at that, everything's showing up to here ... *(He marks the exact spot on the Commendatore's own thigh.)* That smile, that invitation!

COMMENDATORE: But this foot's much more provocative, it's more subtly, more diabolically corrupting ... This little naked foot ... in contrast with the dress, which hides the entire body, and so arouses the imagination ... Don't you agree? *(Raising an eyebrow)* Maybe it's because this girl, this actress, every time I see her ... *(The Commendatore is about to start frothing at the mouth, but he rapidly recovers his composure and leads Mazzuolo to the door.)* In any case, why don't you give me a ring tomorrow, late ... at the office ... We'll see what can be done ... Excuse me, I really must go now, Goodbye...

The Commendatore has opened the door and almost pushes Mazzuolo out.

MAZZUOLO *(still not resigned):* Yes ... but with your support ... Remember ... *It's moral poison!*

The Commendatore closes the door on Mazzuolo's last words. Mazzuolo stands there for a moment, disconcerted and upset. Then, as if attracted by an irresistibly fascinating force, he goes down the few steps leading from the Commendatore's home and gazes out the entrance door.

E.U.R. quarter. Day.

The broiling noonday heat has emptied the streets. The huge billboard insolently dominates the scene. Two little girls stand contemplating it.

Mazzuolo wipes his brow. He is truly in a state of consternation. He looks up and down the sun-bleached street, then hurries away, almost running.

Church. Inside. Day.

Mazzuolo enters the church and hurries toward the sacristy. A huge black coffin rests in the center of the nave, surrounded by tapers. Some workmen up on ladders are hanging black and gold drapes on the walls.

Mazzuolo enters the sacristy.

Sacristy. Day.

Mazzuolo enters the sacristy and comes up to a hunchbacked sexton who is rearranging vestments and other objects.

MAZZUOLO: May I see Monsignor for a moment? ... It's urgent ...

SEXTON: Monsignor's resting ... If you like, sir, I can call the Secretary...

MAZZUOLO: Yes ... Call the Secretary...

Lot with billboard. Day.

A long shiny black limousine pulls up silently below the billboard. Mazzuolo gets out first, then ceremoniously assists the Secretary.

The Secretary is a tall, heavy, impassive-looking man dressed in black.

The sunbaked lot is deserted.

Mazzuolo gestures at the billboard.

MAZZUOLO *(softly):* There it is…

They gaze at the picture in silence.

MAZZUOLO: It needs no comment.

The Secretary makes a vague gesture.

MAZZUOLO: Look at that dress…

Another vague gesture from the Secretary.

MAZZUOLO: The position … Look at the people who pass by here…

But at that moment no one is in sight. The secretary has not even attempted to survey the scene.

MAZZUOLO *(hurrying to clarify):* Well, just now … considering what time it is … But it's usually full of people here … all ages … It's really a pity that Monsignor couldn't come himself, but you'll certainly be able to tell him…

The Secretary nods gravely.

MAZZUOLO: A word from Monsignor would certainly carry the day…

Vague gesture by the Secretary.

MAZZUOLO: I'm sure that when you tell him … when he sees … Monsignor will step in…

As he re-enters the car, the Secretary answers in an expressionless voice:

SECRETARY: We'd already seen this picture …

He makes a vague gesture and disappears inside the enormous car.

Mazzuolo is left speechless …

Mazzuolo's apartment. Bedroom. Day.

The room is submerged in shadow. Mazzuolo, in shirtsleeves, is spying out the half-closed shutters with a pair of binoculars.

His wife is stretched out on the bed, her hair up in a net.

WIFE *(whiningly):* What are you up to, Paolo? Why don't you come take your nap? And you have a headache too...

Mazzuolo does not answer. Now he observes the reactions of the passers-by with indignant attention.

Through the binoculars he sees the curious or amused expressions of some teenagers, of two soldiers, of a young maid waiting for the bus. Now a lengthy file of young girls in boarding-school uniform moves toward the billboard; there are about thirty in all, ten to fifteen years old, chaperoned by a pair of nuns.

At this point Mazzuolo can stand it no longer. He races out of the room.

E.U.R. quarter. Day.

A bottle of ink hits the sign and leaves a small dark splotch as it breaks. The ink rolls down Anita Ekberg's dress. Another bottle of ink follows, then another. As they break, they leave small, insignificant spots on the enormous sign.

Mazzuolo is hurling bottles of ink against the billboard. He is in the throes of a sort of sadistic excitation. His eyes blaze with pleasure.

MAZZUOLO: Take that! ... And that! ... And that!...

Another couple of bottles hit the sign but do very little damage.

A few minutes later. Police-car siren. A crowd has gathered. The Commissioner gets out of a police jeep and looks about inquiringly. The parish priest follows him out of the jeep, and is equally astonished.

The policemen start toward Mazzuolo, who is now hurling rocks at the sign. Finally exhausted, he turns to the officers with a self-satisfied, almost maniacal smile.

MAZZUOLO: Scandal! I'm looking for a scandal! ... *(He throws one last rock.)* That's enough! ... I'm defending the integrity of the family ... The eternal moral values! ... License must stop! ... I'm going to make a scandal!...

The enormous sign is undamaged, save for a few splotches of ink here and there. And Anita's smile is even more shameless.

E.U.R. quarter. Evening.

The sunset is exceptionally lovely; myriad lights are reflected in the waters of the lake. An atmosphere of calm pervades the area.

The billposters' truck is parked beneath the enormous sign. Three or four workmen are up on ladders, partially covering over Anita's figure—her legs, belly, and bosom—with huge gray strips of paper.

The last sheet of paper is plastered over Anita's face. Now the image is unrecognizable. The workmen come down the ladders.

*A man can be seen observing their labors from a balcony in Dr.
Mazzuolo's building. It is Mazzuolo in person, overseeing the
operations.*

Mazzuolo's apartment. Balcony. Evening.

*Out on the balcony, Mazzuolo is following the action through his
binoculars. When Anita's face has been totally concealed, he finally
puts them down. He seems satisfied but also exhausted, pleasantly
exhausted by the victorious battle. There is a certain languor in his
expression.*

He turns to speak to his wife, who is sitting inside, knitting.

MAZZUOLO: That takes care of that. I've done it. We've won.

He is answered by a distant roll of thunder.

Mazzuolo's apartment. Study. Night.

*Mazzuolo sits at his desk working on a speech. He dictates into the
tape recorder, speaking softly so as not to awaken his wife.*

MAZZUOLO: ... I, for instance—and let me not be accused of being
superficial or juvenile—I like Mickey Mouse a very great
deal, and I cite Mickey Mouse for a reason, to exemplify a
type of film which amuses without distracting a man, a
citizen, a father, from his duties and his tasks ... Extremely
delicate tasks they are, too, in an age in which liberty has
been replaced by license, and art by obscenity ... *(Pause)* The
cinema ... *(He clears his throat.)* The cinema must offer
tranquil intermissions of rest and of amusement. It must offer
a valid contribution in this difficult life ... in this difficult
daily life we must make our way through, among the
constant temptations ... that is, no, among the constant
spiritual and material dangers which threaten mankind ...
(Pause; then, in conclusion) which threaten mankind.

*Weary now, Mazzuolo runs the tape back to listen to what he has
dictated.*

A sudden crash of thunder. Mazzuolo starts. The thunder dies down. Mazzuolo looks toward the window. Raindrops are beginning to beat against the windowpanes.

MAZZUOLO: Hm, it's raining.

Another crash of thunder. Mazzuolo stops the tape and listens to the playback.

TAPE: ... high and noble sentiments ... *(He runs the tape further back.)* ... comprehension and fraternity ... *(He runs the tape still further back. But evidently he has gone too far this time: his tone-deaf voice is now singing.)* Your heart is of ice ... Of ice...

He immediately stops the tape and glances about, as if fearing that someone may discover his weakness for song.

Another crash of thunder. Now the rain is pouring down. Mazzuolo goes to the window to watch the rain, then returns to the tape recorder and starts the tape again.

TAPE: "Ladies and gentlemen, it is painful but necessary to admit that we live in an age ruled by the senses and by matter ... An era in which..."

An exceptionally loud crash of thunder drowns out the recording. Mazzuolo turns the machine off and reads over what he has written. He hears a noise, perhaps a door creaking on its hinges, and looks up.

MAZZUOLO: Who's there? *(But he hears only the sound of the rain. Tensely)* Who's there? Come in? Is that you, Adele?

Silence. He turns back to his papers. The noise is repeated. Mazzuolo cannot identify its origin. He goes out into the hall and searches everywhere for the source of the sound. But now all is still.

Mazzuolo returns to his study. Silence. He goes to the window and looks out at the sign. He is stunned to see that the rain has loosened the gray sheets of paper masking Anita's image, and that they are slowly being washed off the billboard.

He watches in utter fascination as Anita triumphantly reemerges through the rain.

Anita's face. Now Anita moves her head and fixes her eyes directly on Mazzuolo.

Mazzuolo steps back, then immediately returns to the window and discovers that Anita has turned her back on him.

A sort of moan escapes Mazzuolo's lips; then, with the courage of desperation, he rushes into the hall, catches up his umbrella and softly opens the door. He listens to make sure that no one is awake, then slips out like a thief in the night.

E.U.R. quarter. Night.

The rain is gradually letting up. Protected by his umbrella, Mazzuolo leaves the building and heads for the huge billboard, which can be seen dimly across the open lot.

And owl hoots lugubriously.

Mazzuolo stops and looks through the trees. There is a faintly menacing quality to the night. Rain drips from the trees.

The rain stops suddenly. Mazzuolo lowers his umbrella, holds out his palm to check, then closes the umbrella.

He approaches the billboard. Her back still turned on him, Anita's figure is reflected in the waters of the nearby pond. Suddenly she turns, stretches and yawns. She seems to wish to go to sleep. She closes her eyes and rests her head on her hands.

Mazzuolo stands about twenty yards in front of the sign, where he can take it all in at once. He hesitates to come any closer. Then he plucks up his courage and starts forward, cautiously, shaking as if caught in an incredible dream.

Now the figure of Anita looms over him.

She slowly opens her eyes and stares at Mazzuolo: a motionless, implacable stare.

Mazzuolo slowly pulls back under that nightmarish gaze. Her eyes follow him.

A voice—Anita's voice—resounds through the night:

ANITA: Excuse me. Excuse me, darling. Can I just ask you one thing?...

Pale as death, Mazzuolo freezes in his steps. He is speechless.

ANITA: It won't hurt if I just talk to you, will it? ... In a ladylike way. Just one word.

Anita begins to comb her sumptuous locks.

MAZZUOLO *(stammering):* To me? ...

ANITA: Don't be scared, darling. Are you scared? Do I frighten you so? ... Come here...

Mazzuolo draws himself up.

MAZZUOLO *(with a choked, ironically aggressive voice):* Scared? ... Me? ... Go on, what is it?...

ANITA: What kind of a tone of voice is that?

MAZZUOLO *(more confident and aggressive now):* Go on, what is it? ... We know what you want to say! ... Go on, go on, I'll have my say afterward!...

ANITA: I just wanted to ask you, in a very ladylike way, without throwing any bottles of ink around at anybody, what have you got against me? You don't give me a minute's peace. What's so bad about what I'm doing? Have I bothered anybody? I don't do a thing up here. I just lie here ... like a cloud. Is that so terrible, a pretty cloud? ... A beautiful big cloud? I take the sun, I look around...

MAZZUOLO *(breaking into a shrill, sardonic cackle):* The innocence of nature, eh? ... Clouds, sun ... Sweden ... Who do you take me for? You think you can make me fall for that kind of stuff? There're clouds and clouds, my girl! Even some clouds can resemble shapes that I needn't mention now ... the purity of creation! ... Nothing's pure, my girl ... You make me laugh!

He laughs once more, harshly and somewhat hysterically. His laughter is suddenly echoed by Anita's, which explodes unexpectedly, bloodcurdling despite her cordial tone. Mazzuolo shudders in horror.

MAZZUOLO *(with mixed aggressiveness and terror):* What's so funny?...

ANITA: You laughed, so I laughed too. What's the matter, can't I even laugh? I have a cheerful disposition, you know...

To overcome his terror, Mazzuolo now explodes in violent abuse, all a-tremor with sanctimonious indignation.

MAZZUOLO: No! ... I can laugh. Not you? Your laugh is cynical or irresponsible! ... You haven't any right to laugh at decent people! You think it's so easy to be decent and pure? It's much easier to be licentious, like you are! For shame! ... Do you have any idea of the ruinous effect you have on people? on the family? on Society? ... Ah, you're just taking the sun, eh? ... Enjoying the scenery? ... You liar! ... I'll shout it right to your face: liar, hypocrite, corrupter of morals! ... You're sowing ruin and scandal! ... If so many decent people go wrong ... if there's so much evil in this world of ours, so wanting in faith and hope, it's your fault!...

An enormous tear plunges down from on high, forming a little puddle on the ground beside Mazzuolo. Then another, and another. Sidestepping to avoid them, Mazzuolo goes on, his face flushed with wrath.

MAZZUOLO: ... You're crying? ... Cry, cry, it'll do you good! ... I'm glad I made you cry! ... At last I've been able to confront you face to face ... give you a moral whipping ... Weep, weep!

He opens his umbrella as the huge tears continue to shower down around him.

Anita's voice, now weepy, warns him in a friendly way.

ANITA: Be careful ... Move back ... It's full of mascara ... It'll leave a stain, and your wife ... Just look who I have to meet up with! ... A guy who doesn't even enjoy the sight of a nice-looking girl!... *(Mazzuolo starts to answer, but Anita hurries to ward him off.)* All right, all right, take it easy, you're perfectly right! ... God, what a bore! ... You're right, just stop it now. You're giving me a headache! ... Got a cigarette?

MAZZUOLO: No! ... I don't smoke!

ANITA: That's too bad! ... Well then, how should I be?

Anita is changing position now. Fascinated and distraught, Mazzuolo does not fully understand.

MAZZUOLO: You're asking me? ... I ... Why?...

ANITA: Come on ... You tell me. I'll do whatever you say, all right? ... How should I be?...

Mazzuolo stares in fascination at Anita's movements. Now, his voice somewhat more relaxed but still energetic (even overly so). He orders:

MAZZUOLO: Decorous. Decorous and decently covered.

Anita tries to pull her dress down over her legs, and rearranges her neckline.

ANITA: Like this?

MAZZUOLO: No ... No ...

ANITA: Well how, like this?

MAZZUOLO *(distraught and stammering):* For the love of God! Decorous ... decent ... Back ... Further back!

ANITA: What?

MAZZUOLO: That leg ... No! That other thing ... The ... The...

ANITA: The thigh?

MAZZUOLO: That thing there ... Further back! The dress higher up
    ... Cover yourself! ... Further down ... No, that's enough!
    Further up!

ANITA: I just did what you said! You're confusing me! Oh!

*One of Anita's shoes slips off and crashes to the ground beside
Mazzuolo, who barely manages to jump out of the way.*

MAZZUOLO *(still distraught, but more aggressive):* Then wear a

longer dress, less tight! If you cover up one part it uncovers another ... You can pull as much as you want to; if the cloth's not there, it's not there.

Anita lowers her enormous leg out of the sign and searches with it for her shoe. Suddenly she sits up, her face now irate. Her voice becomes cutting.

ANITA: You know what I think? ... You've made me sore.

The foot has found its shoe and slipped into it. Now the other leg descends beside it and Anita stands up, towering gigantically above Mazzuolo. Her skirts cascade over him like an enormous bell, completely concealing him from sight.

Suffocating and terrified, Mazzuolo struggles wildly through the silken folds, searching for a way out. A sea of lace, nylon, and billowing silk envelops his head and hinders his movements. Anita's laughter echoes through the night again, somewhat menacing in tone now.

MAZZUOLO: You shameless creature! ... Let me out! ... Demon!...

Anita suddenly picks up her skirts and pirouettes away, still laughing. The deserted boulevards and the surrealistic, white buildings echo her laughter and magnify it.

ANITA: I dress like I want to, I lie like I want to, and I show what I want to!...

Leaping and twirling about, Anita goes off down the boulevard. Now her voice resounds with an unnatural, almost sinister quality as she turns to shout to Mazzuolo.

ANITA: And to whom I like!...

Maddened, Mazzuolo starts to run breathlessly after her, shouting in a choked voice.

MAZZUOLO: Shameless woman! ... Corrupter! ... Away! ... Away with you!...

Anita has disappeared around a corner.

But suddenly, just as Mazzuolo is about to reach the corner, her head reappears, making him jump back.

ANITA: Why should I listen to you, you don't even know what a woman is!...

MAZZUOLO *(screaming hysterically):* Away! ... Get away from here!...

Laughing, Anita disappears.

Mazzuolo races around the corner and sees her a little further on, leaping and splashing through the puddles. She plunges her foot into the water to splash Mazzuolo as he runs up.

ANITA: Come on, do you know? ... Do you know what a woman is? You don't know anything! ... You're still sixteen years old, and you think everybody else is just like you...

She starts off again, running, with Mazzuolo chasing wildly after her. She disappears behind another building. He hears her laughing.

ANITA: You're a poor little man! ... A poor little thing! ... I feel sorry for you!...

MAZZUOLO: Away with you! ... I'll drive you away! ... away, corrupter!...

As he rounds the corner, Mazzuolo sees Anita standing against the high white stairway of another huge building. She seems to be waiting for him. He stops short, panting, frozen by the starkness of that sight.

ANITA: I feel sorry for you, mister. Sorry and angry. Can you possibly be so upset by the sight of a naked woman? ... Well, I'm going to get naked right now!...

Slowly Anita removes the scarf from her shoulders and throws it to the ground as if commencing a rite.

MAZZUOLO *(screaming hoarsely):* No! ... Don't you dare! ... I forbid it!...

*Without answering, Anita unfastens her dress with the same slow,
ritualistic gestures.*

*Mazzuolo seems to have gone mad. He looks wildly about, seizes the
pole of a large café parasol, and brandishes the steel tip toward the
woman.*

MAZZUOLO: Don't you dare! ... Look out!...

Anita lets her shoulder strap slip down over her arm.

Brandishing his pole, Mazzuolo prances about as if on horseback. His head is encased in a plumed helmet; shining armor girds his body.

MAZZUOLO: Stop! ... Stop, demon!...

Then, with an even hoarser cry, he hurls the pole with all his might.

MAZZUOLO: ... Out of this world, demon!...

A crash is heard.

The pole has lodged in the billboard at the exact point of the heart of the woman lying still there.

Mazzuolo is standing stock-still at the base of the billboard, helmetless and unarmored, his eyes staring at the image. His face is transfixed and bathed in sweat; he is panting heavily.

The pole vibrates to and fro in the billboard, with a faint twanging sound.

There is a sinister silence around Mazzuolo. A huge shadow has covered the moon. From the far end of the long deserted boulevard, two rows of gigantic tapers advance slowly through the dark, borne in silent procession by files of monk-hooded men.

Eight pairs of big black horses, caparisoned in black, advance at a slow walk.

MAZZUOLO *(shudders and stammers):* No ... no...

He tries to reach the pole implanted in the billboard. He rises up on tiptoes. He cannot reach it. He tries to climb up on the scaffolding; he slips down ...

The black procession of hooded men and horses continues its slow advance...

Lot with billboard. Day.

It is a rainy morning. An ambulance siren is heard approaching. The Fire Department ambulance appears and stops in front of the billboard. A crowd of about a hundred people—many with umbrellas—has gathered about to watch.

Mazzuolo is standing on the upper edge of the billboard. His collar is up; he shivers with the cold.

The crowd watches in silence. Adele, his wife, is there too, weeping softly and comforted by several women. A number of policemen stand around with the Commissioner. Meanwhile, the firemen have raised their ladder to the top of the billboard and one of them climbs up and tries to induce the undaunted Mazzuolo to come down. He seems not to notice either the crowd or all these operations; he stares straight ahead, bitter and desperate.

The fireman is now nearing Mazzuolo.

FIREMAN *(calmly, softly):* Come on, come on down, be a good fellow … Come on down, then you can go back up again when you want to … even right away … It's just a formality…

Mazzuolo climbs down to the fireman. Other firemen surround the two and help them the rest of the way down. Adele runs toward Mazzuolo.

ADELE *(crying):* Paolo!

Mazzuolo stares blankly at her. Docile now, he enters the ambulance, still staring at the image of the woman on the sign.

On the billboard, Anita's image seems to be following him with a quizzical gaze.

The ambulance roars off. Up on the roof, a small winged cupid is having some trouble keeping his balance, but he laughs, grabs his foot with one hand, rolls over and sits up again, reeling…

He laughs again—the same little giggle we have heard before…

CUPID: That's what I was saying: if I lose my temper, it always ends up catra-catatra-catastrophically!

THE END